Sue—

May your ~
with Holy
grow s~
each new

In His
Mary Lou

Listening to the voice of God is a learned art, not a gift. I know of no better way to learn this art than reflecting on the words of the Holy Spirit to a seasoned listener such as Jennifer. As you glean from her listening ear and watchful heart you too will learn to recognize the voice of your faithful teacher and friend, the Holy Spirit.

—DUTCH SHEETS
INTERNATIONAL PRAYER LEADER
AND CONFERENCE SPEAKER,
AUTHOR, *APPEAL TO HEAVEN*

Not a day goes by that I do not talk to the Holy Spirit, whether it is in my natural language or my prayer language. Our conversations are profound, personal, and filled with promise. He promises He'll never leave me and walks with me through trials and temptations, through joy and sorrow. I encourage you to invite Him in to every area of your life, and you'll see a difference. *Mornings With the Holy Spirit* provides quick reminders of how the Holy Spirit longs to dwell within you daily.

—DR. MARILYN HICKEY
PRESIDENT AND FOUNDER,
MARILYN HICKEY MINISTRIES

In *Mornings With the Holy Spirit* Jennifer LeClaire offers us a glimpse into the intimacy with God that is possible even now. He longs to have a deep, personal relationship with all believers because He delights in us. This inspiring devotional will encourage you to walk with Him, talk with Him, and love Him with all your heart, mind, soul, and strength.

—MIKE BICKLE
DIRECTOR, INTERNATIONAL HOUSE OF
PRAYER, KANSAS CITY

Want to start each day off with a burning word in your heart and put the glow of the Holy Spirit upon your life? Then look no further! Inspirational words from Jennifer LeClaire are for you. Start the first day of the rest of your life off right!

—DR. JAMES W. GOLL
ENCOUNTERS NETWORK, PRAYER STORM,
GET eSchool, INTERNATIONAL BEST-
SELLING AUTHOR

MORNINGS

WITH THE

*Holy
Spirit*

JENNIFER LeCLAIRE

CHARISMA
HOUSE

Most Charisma House Book Group products
are available at special quantity discounts for bulk
purchase for sales promotions, premiums, fund-
raising, and educational needs. For details, write
Charisma House Book Group, 600 Rinehart Road,
Lake Mary, Florida 32746, or telephone (407)
333-0600.

Mornings With the Holy Spirit
   by Jennifer LeClaire
Published by Charisma House
Charisma Media/Charisma House Book Group
600 Rinehart Road
Lake Mary, Florida 32746
www.charismahouse.com

Unless otherwise noted, all Scripture quotations are
taken from the Modern English Version. Copyright
© 2014 by Military Bible Association. Used by
permission. All rights reserved.

Scripture quotations marked AMP are from the
Amplified Bible. Copyright © 1954, 1958, 1962,

Cover design by Lisa Rae Cox
Design Director: Justin Evans

Visit the author's website at www.jenniferleclaire.org.

Library of Congress Cataloging-in-Publication Data:
LeClaire, Jennifer (Jennifer L.)
  Mornings with the Holy Spirit / by Jennifer
LeClaire. -- First edition.
     pages cm
  ISBN 978-1-62998-189-5 (hardcover) -- ISBN
978-1-62998-190-1 (e-book)
 1. Devotional calendars. 2. Holy Spirit--
Miscellanea. I. Title.
  BV4811.L43 2015
  242'.2--dc23

                                    2014036807

21 22 23 24 — 9 8 7 6
Printed in Canada

I dedicate this book to my daughter, Bridgette, a precious gift from God who taught me how to love unconditionally and inspired me to lay down my life for another. Her heart is quick to forgive, her joy is contagious, and her perseverance is an example of how Christ strengthens us to do all things when we pursue His will. I can't imagine my life without the opportunity to raise this beautiful young woman. I love you, Bridgette, and God loves you even more than I do.

I RAN FROM GOD for many years before I finally surrendered to His will, but clear evidence proves His hand was on my life even when I was running in the opposite direction. In fact, when my husband abandoned me in 1999 with a two-year-old baby, I shook my fist at God and demanded answers for the injustice. He was silent then, but I know now He was watching over me and protecting me. His thoughts toward me were thoughts of peace and not of evil, to give me a future and a hope (Jer. 29:11).

About eighteen months after my husband disappeared and left our lives in shambles, I was arrested for a crime I didn't commit. I was facing five years in prison—a sentence that would have left my daughter essentially orphaned. Helpless and hopeless, I finally cried out to God—and He delivered me from the enemy's plot to destroy our lives. Wearing a bright orange jumpsuit in a dark county jail, I surrendered my heart to the One who created me, and the peace of God that passes all understanding guarded my heart and mind in Christ Jesus (Phil. 4:7).

It was in this setting—a county jail filled with prostitutes, drug addicts, thieves, and all manner of violent criminals—that I heard the still, small voice of God for the first time. In this place of captivity I discovered that where the Spirit of the Lord is, there is liberty (2 Cor. 3:17). In the face of impossibility God taught me that all things are possible to Him who believes (Mark 9:23).

I'll never forget my experience. The Holy Spirit showed me in the Word and spoke to my heart that I would be released in forty days. Being a new convert, I had no idea that the number forty was a symbol of testing and trial, but every time I opened my Bible, I read an account that revolved around that number: Moses's forty years in Egypt, the Israelites' forty years in the desert, Noah's experience with the forty-day flood, Jesus's forty days in the wilderness.

After several days of supernatural guidance through the Word, the Holy Spirit made it clear to my heart that I would be released from the injustice of imprisonment in forty days. It seemed impossible, considering that the judge had refused to allow me bail three times—and that this same judge was on vacation well after the fortieth day of my captivity. All I can say is, "But God." On the fortieth day I was called into a holding cell with other inmates. I was never tried or convicted by my accusers. I never stood before an earthly judge. Thankfully, *the* judge—Jesus Christ—is not a man that He should lie. I was released on the fortieth day, just as the Holy Spirit told me I would be.

That was the beginning of a beautiful friendship with the Holy Spirit that has opened the door for me to receive all His benefits: His leading, His guidance, His revelation, His comfort, His truth, His grace, and much more. The Holy Spirit is so faithful! He never fails to speak to my heart at critical moments. He is quick to warn me when I am heading down the wrong path. He graciously offers the wisdom I need to overcome any obstacle. And He always has a word for me in due season when I am careful to maintain a listening ear and a watchful heart.

God has restored my life in beautiful ways, more than making up for the injustice of being abandoned with a baby as well as being falsely accused and imprisoned. Today I serve as a senior editor at *Charisma* magazine, a cutting-edge periodical published by one of the largest Christian media companies in the world. I have authored more than a dozen books, ministered in several nations, and appeared on many TV and radio broadcasts. I also direct a thriving prayer ministry in Fort Lauderdale, Florida. Most importantly, I have a special relationship with my wonderful daughter, who has weathered the storms of life with me.

As my relationship with the Holy Spirit has developed through the years, I've learned plenty about how He speaks and what He likes to talk about. If you're listening, it's not difficult to hear Him. He communicates through faint impressions, dreams, visions, circumstances, nature, other people—and of course through Scripture. Most of the time, though, He speaks in the still, small voice I first heard in the county jail. He uses it to commune with us about His favorite subjects: Father God, Jesus, and us.

The Holy Spirit likes to talk about Father. He likes to talk about Jesus. He likes to talk about His love for us; His enjoyment of us; and His desire to help us, teach us, comfort us, pray with us, empower us, and guide us into truth—about God and about ourselves. He likes to woo us into His presence. He likes to engage our hearts in conversation and in worship.

I imagine the disciples were shocked when Jesus told them it was better for them that He go away because unless He ascended to the Father, the

Holy Spirit would not come to them (John 16:7). At that point the disciples didn't have a relationship with the Holy Spirit, so they didn't know what they were missing. But Jesus realized that without the Holy Spirit, His followers—including us—would not be able to fulfill God's call on their lives. So He sent the Holy Spirit to be our helper, our teacher, our Comforter, our Advocate, our intercessor, our strengthener, the One who empowers us, the revealer of truth, and our standby. (See John 14–16, AMP.)

The Bible confirms that the Holy Spirit is the third person of the Godhead, co-equal with the Father and the Son (Acts 5:3–4). He is the co-Creator of the universe (Gen. 1:1–3) and the author of Scripture (2 Tim. 3:16). He is omnipresent (Ps. 139:7–10), omniscient (1 Cor. 2:9 11), and omnipotent, just as the other two persons are (Luke 1:35; Rom. 15:19). He is the One who overshadowed Mary and caused her to conceive Jesus in human form (Matt. 1:18; Luke 1:35), and He will glorify Christ forever (John 16:14).

Developing a relationship with the Holy Spirit is crucial for those who desire to discover and fulfill God's will for their lives. He does so much for us! Just take a look at this list.

The Holy Spirit:

+ Loves us (Rom. 15:30)

+ Regenerates and renews our souls (Titus 3:4–5)

+ Convicts us of sin (John 16:7–9)

+ Teaches us (Neh. 9:20; John 14:26)

+ Guides us into truth (John 16:13)

+ Leads us (Rom. 8:14)

+ Reveals to us the things God has prepared for us (1 Cor. 2:9–10)

+ Speaks *to* us (John 15:26; 16:13–15; Acts 8:29; 10:19; 11:12; 13:2; 16:6–7; 1 Tim. 4:1; Heb. 3:7; Rev. 2:7, 11, 17, 29; 3:6, 13, 22) and *through* us (Matt. 10:20; 1 Cor. 12:3; 14:2; Acts 2:4; 11:28; 21:4, 11)

+ Prays through us (Rom. 8:26)

+ Transforms us into the image of Christ (2 Cor. 3:18)

+ Causes us to manifest His fruit—love, joy, peace, patience, kindness, goodness, faithfulness, gentleness, and self-control—as we walk in the Spirit rather than in the flesh (Gal. 5:16–23)

- Endues us with Christ's power (Acts 1:8)
- Gives us spiritual gifts (1 Cor. 12:1–11; Heb. 2:4)
- Anoints us for ministry (Luke 4:18)

The Holy Spirit does all this for us and much more. And though He is able to make His voice heard to anyone at any time, truly knowing Him requires consistently tuning one's ear to His still, small voice and following His leading.

I wrote this book because I'm aware that many Christians who are on fire for God and love Jesus with all their hearts, minds, souls, and strength are less familiar with the Holy Spirit. I get e-mails from people all over the world who long to fellowship with the Spirit of God and hear His still, small voice but don't know how or don't believe they can. I get messages from people desperate for the Holy Spirit's edification, exhortation, comfort, leading, and guidance. Some haven't learned to tune into His voice amid the chaos of life. Others miss His words because they aren't familiar with what His still, small voice sounds like and the types of things He says.

As much as I'd like to, I can't teach them— one by one—how to still their souls and listen for the voice of the Holy Spirit that will speak life-changing truth and practical guidance day by day. But through this book I can share with many of you the inspiring words He has spoken to my heart in the hope that they will not only motivate you but also equip you with the prophetic exhortation and scriptural backing you need to press in to God to satisfy your hunger and thirst for more.

This daily devotional contains prophetic words the Holy Spirit spoke to my heart day by day as I spent time with Him. These words have encouraged me when I felt like giving up, inspired me to rise up and fight for what Christ has given me, moved my heart with a revelation of the great love our heavenly Father has for me, and so much more. I pray that they also speak to your heart, stir your faith, and cause you to press in to hear God for yourself. He wants to speak to you personally and fellowship with you intimately. As you read and reflect on the entries daily, write down what you sense the Holy Spirit is saying to you—beyond what you see on the pages of this book. Then use His words to encourage others and inspire them to spend time in His presence, learning to hear His still, small voice as you have.

—JENNIFER LECLAIRE

January

"In the last days it shall be," says God, "that I will pour out My Spirit on all flesh; your sons and your daughters shall prophesy, your young men shall see visions, and your old men shall dream dreams. Even on My menservants and maidservants I will pour out My Spirit in those days."

—ACTS 2:17–18

DETERMINE TO FOLLOW YOUR DESIRES

ETERMINE TO FOLLOW your desires, for I have placed those desires in your heart as you have delighted yourself in Father. As you continue to seek first the kingdom and Our righteousness, I will direct your steps on a lighted path that will take you where we both want you to go. Apart from Christ you can do nothing, but you are not apart from Christ. You are in Christ, and He is in you. If you determine to reach His high calling for you and lean and depend on Me to guide you, nothing shall by any means stop you.

PSALM 37:4; MATTHEW 6:33; PROVERBS 3:5

→ PRAYER ←

*Thank You for Your faithfulness to the dreams
You have put in my heart. Give me a determined heart that will not turn to the right or
to the left. Help me to stay focused on Your
perfect will for me this day and every day.*

January 2

I Love to Hear You Pray

I LOVE TO HEAR your voice in prayer every morning when you awake. It's one of My favorite parts of the day. When you awake and begin declaring your love for Us, it moves Our heart. When you inquire of Me, it is My pleasure to answer. When you speak to My heart, it is My joy to speak back to yours. I hear your voice even when the hectic pace of life makes it difficult for you to hear Mine. So keep lifting your voice to Father in prayer. Keep telling Me about your struggles and fears and dreams and victories. I'm listening.

PSALM 63:1; PSALM 27:4; PSALM 34:15

→ PRAYER ←

Remind me to begin each day praising Your name and lifting up my petitions to Father's throne—and help me because I do not know how to pray as I ought. I trust in You to help me touch Father's heart in prayer.

WHO DO YOU SAY THAT I AM?

*J*ESUS ONCE ASKED His disciples, "Who do you say that I am?" Many people knew He was a great prophet, but only Peter received the revelation that He was the Christ, the Son of the living God. Now, I ask you, who do you say that I am? Many people disregard My work in their lives because they don't understand who I am. And even those who know Me don't always have a continual awareness of My presence and a deep revelation of My love for them. Who do you say that I am? Search My heart, and I will show you a new realm of My faithfulness, My kindness, and so much more. Search My heart.

LUKE 9:18–21; ISAIAH 11:2; GALATIANS 5:22–23

✦ PRAYER ✦

Holy Spirit, I know what Jesus said about You, and I've read about You in Scripture, but I want to know You more and more—experientially. I want to experience who You are in a fresh way. Help me to search Your heart, and show me more about Yourself.

January 4

LOOK AHEAD TO YOUR DESTINY

Don't look back. I know your hurts. I know your wounds. I know your disappointments. I saw the betrayals. I saw the tears. I was with you through the pain, and I am here to make it right. I will work it all—the hurt, the disappointment, the betrayals—together for your good because you love Me and I love you. I will give you beauty for ashes. But you have to leave those ashes behind so I can resurrect with newness of life those things the enemy tried to steal, kill, and destroy.

Remember Lot's wife. Don't look back. Your destiny is ahead, and I am leading you toward your dreams.

PHILIPPIANS 3:12–14; ISAIAH 61:3; ROMANS 8:28

→ PRAYER ←

Thank You for Your healing power in my soul. Give me the strength to press beyond the past and toward my high calling in Christ. Show me how to make the divine exchange that will give me beauty for ashes, and I will glorify Your name.

I Can Do More Than You Can Imagine

*T*AKE THE LIMITS off. Do you realize that the power that raised Christ Jesus from the dead dwells in you? Do you know that I am able to do more—much, much more—for you than you can ever imagine? Do you know that I *want* to? Will you believe in Me the way I believe in you?

Take the limits off! Dream with Me! Let your eyes see, your ears hear, and your heart dwell on what I have prepared for the one I love. Your best is yet to come. Only believe.

EPHESIANS 1:19–20; EPHESIANS 3:20;
1 CORINTHIANS 2:9

✦ PRAYER ✦

Your promises are glorious, and I want to walk in every one of them. I want to see things the way You see them. Reveal to me the things You have prepared for me in love. Stir my heart to follow You toward Your perfect will.

YOUR WEAKNESS DOES
NOT DISAPPOINT ME

I KNOW YOU FEEL weak on some days. Rejoice! My strength is made perfect in your weakness. Your weakness does not surprise Me or disappoint Me. I knew that you would not always win your inner battles with temptation when I wooed you into this relationship. You are a work in progress, but I see you as a masterpiece despite your failures. I see you as a winner! I see you through the eyes of love. I see you through the blood of Jesus. So call upon Me to strengthen you, and I will help you overcome your weaknesses.

2 CORINTHIANS 12:9; EPHESIANS 2:10;
EPHESIANS 3:16

✦ PRAYER ✦

*I'm so glad that nothing can separate me
from Your love. Strengthen me in my inner
man so I can resist all the temptations of
the evil one. And help me see myself the
way You see me—complete in Christ.*

I Love You Just the Way You Are

You don't have to try to be someone you are not. I love you just the way you were created. Don't compare yourself to anyone else. I have given you unique gifts and talents, and I have called you for such a time as this. If you allow frustration to flood your heart, you only hinder My grace. So reject comparisons. Reject frustrations. Reject striving. Embrace who you are now. Move forward as the person I've called you to be, and your unique gifts will make room for you.

1 John 4:8; 2 Corinthians 10:12;
1 Corinthians 12

→ Prayer ←

You see into my heart in ways that I don't see myself. Help me not to compare myself to others or give in to the frustrations of daily life. Help me to rest in You instead of striving. Show me how to do things Your way instead of my way.

Don't Doubt!

*D*OUBT IS THE doorway to unbelief. Doubt is a cousin of fear and suspicion, and it blocks discernment. The enemy wants you to walk in the curse of doubt. He wants you to worry day and night. But Jesus came to redeem you from the curse. Father has given you the measure of faith that opens the doorway to His promises. Resist doubt as you would resist the devil, and let your faith rise as you meditate on the blessings I've promised you.

GALATIANS 3:13; ROMANS 12:3; JOSHUA 1:8

✦ PRAYER ✦

*Show me when doubt is trying to enter my soul.
Give me a discerning spirit so I can recognize
the enemy's attempts to muddy my faith with
his lies. I submit myself to You. Give me the
strength to resist the devil so that he will flee.*

IT'S NEVER TOO LATE TO START OVER

*N*O MATTER WHAT destruction the enemy has brought to your life, you can start over again. Father started over with Noah after the destruction of the Flood. He made a covenant with man never to flood the earth again. And He has made a covenant with you through His Son. So be at peace, knowing that when the enemy comes in like a flood, Father will raise up a standard against him. And what the enemy meant for harm, Father means for good. You can start again in My grace. It's never too late to start over in Christ.

GENESIS 9:17; ISAIAH 59:19; GENESIS 50:20

→ PRAYER ←

Thank You for Your covenant with me. Thank You for protecting me from the wiles of the enemy. Thank You for giving me a fresh start in Christ. Anoint me to walk out of the old season and into what You have planned for me.

January 10

I Want to Help You

I know it's too hard for you, but it's not too hard for Me. I want to help you. I am your helper, and I find joy in coming alongside you, sharing My strength, showing you things to come, and giving you the right words to say. I know sometimes things look impossible and you can't see the way out or the way through. But I know the way: His name is Jesus. I'm here to lead you and guide you, so follow Me, and the confusion and stress will give way to clarity and peace.

JEREMIAH 32:27; JOHN 14:26; JOHN 16:13

✦ PRAYER ✦

Holy Spirit, I need Your peace. I need Your strength. I need Your guidance. Please help me become more sensitive to Your leading at every turn, and flood my soul with confidence in Christ and the peace of God that passes all understanding. I am willing to follow You.

I AM YOUR DEVOTED ONE

*E*VEN THOSE LITTLE moments when you think of Me ravish My heart. You are My devoted one, and I am your devoted One. I have eyes only for you, and when you so much as look My way, it thrills My heart. Our fellowship is My delight. Your voice is like a sweet melody in My ears. I am always in Your presence, and you are always in Mine. Together, we can do anything. I am your Grace. You are Our beloved.

PSALM 17:8; SONG OF SONGS 1:13–16

→ PRAYER ←

*I've never known anyone as beautiful as You.
Will You keep me as the apple of Your eye?
Will You hide me in the shadow of Your wings?
Protect me and keep me, and I will lavish my
love upon You. You are worthy of my all.*

January 12

I WILL REVEAL JESUS TO YOU

It's My joy to reveal Jesus to your heart. He loves you with a passionate love. He is always interceding for you to Father. And He always has a word of comfort and strength to share with you. I want you to know Him the way I know Him. Will you allow Me to make more of Him known to you through His Word? Open the Gospels in faith, and I will pour out a spirit of wisdom and revelation in the knowledge of Jesus. As we gaze upon His beauty together, you will be transformed into His image.

EPHESIANS 1:17; PSALM 27:4;
2 CORINTHIANS 3:18

✦ PRAYER ✦

Your promises overwhelm me, and I say yes!
Give me revelation and wisdom in the knowl-
edge of Jesus. Show me Your glory. Show
me Your beauty. Fix my eyes on Your heart.
Help me to focus on You and You alone.

YOU CAN TELL ME ANYTHING

*Y*OU CAN TRUST Me. I am your confidant. I am your counselor. You can tell Me anything. Share your God-given dreams with Me, and I will help you bring them to pass. Share your fears with Me, and I will help you overcome them. Share your prayers with Me, and I will help you lift them to Father. You can trust Me. Seeing you walk in everything Jesus has for you—helping you reach your destiny in Christ—is part of My mission. I am on your side! I am for you, not against you.

JOHN 14:26; ROMANS 8:26; ROMANS 8:31

→ PRAYER ←

I need Your help more than I realized. Please hear my heart and help me to lean and depend on You as the lover of my soul. Deliver me from evil, and help me become all Jesus died and rose again for me to be. Help me to trust You more.

January 14

I Will Give You Wisdom and Strategies for Victory

J UST AS I was with Moses and Joshua and David, empowering them with wisdom and revelation and delivering them from the hand of the enemy, so I am with you. I am the power that defeats all your enemies. Speak against your spiritual foes in the name of Jesus, and I will enforce His will against your enemies—they will fall in defeat. I will give you wisdom for every battle and reveal strategies for victory. Just as I was with Moses and Joshua and David, so I am with you.

ZECHARIAH 4:6; PSALM 31:8; PSALM 24:8

＞ Prayer ＜

Give me a revelation of Your presence and an understanding of the power of the name of Jesus that I may stand confidently—fearlessly—against the wiles of the enemy and see Your victory in my life. Thank You for the authority to use Christ's name!

I AM WAITING TO REVEAL TRUTH

I AM NEARER THAN you think. I am closer than you know. I am always with you—waiting. I am waiting for you to engage in a conversation with Me. I want to show you things to come. I desire to reveal more of Jesus and Father to you. I love it when you ask Me questions because it is My joy to lead you into all truth. I am right here. I have all knowledge. What do you want to know? Ask Me in faith. I will lead you and guide you to the information and revelation you desire.

JOHN 16:13; JAMES 1:5; MATTHEW 7:7

✤ PRAYER ✤

You are the revealer of truth and the giver of wisdom. Will You give me the wisdom to ask You what I really need to know? Show me what to ask, and I will grow in Your wisdom and joy. I am open to receiving Your wise counsel in every area of my life.

January 16

PREPARE FOR A NEW SEASON

I'VE GIVEN YOU a gift, and I expect you to use it. You've wondered many times why your gift has not made room for you. But, My friend, you must take the first step and make room for the gift. You must put away from you and lay aside those things that are distracting you from My higher purpose for your life. I want to take you into deep waters. Prepare yourself now for a new season in which My gifts will manifest through you for the glory of Christ.

PROVERBS 18:16; 1 CORINTHIANS 13:11;
HEBREWS 12:1

→ PRAYER ←

I want to glorify Christ with the gifts You've given me. I will yield to Your Spirit if You make Your way known to me. Help me to turn away from anything and everything that's distracting me from Your love, Your presence, and Your will.

DON'T ALLOW PEOPLE TO DISTRACT YOU

*E*VALUATE YOUR LIFE. When you take time to reflect on your relationships, it becomes easy to see who is supporting you and who is distracting you from Father's will. Know this: the enemy of your soul is on assignment to hinder your destiny. He often works through people—sometimes even people you like. The enemy uses people you don't know as well as people who are close to you to pull your attention away from Our will. Love the people. They don't know the enemy is using them. But don't be deceived. Stay focused on what Father has called you to do.

JOHN 10:10; EPHESIANS 5:2; JAMES 1:22

✦ PRAYER ✦

Help me stay focused on You and Your will for my life and not on what people think I should do. Please give me discernment to recognize when the enemy is using the voices of people around me to distract me from Your true direction.

January 18

Forget What Lies Behind

*I*T'S A NEW day. Forget what lies behind, and press on to what Jesus has for you. Don't let your mind wander to the people and places of the past, no matter how good or how bad. If you try to move forward while looking back, you will stumble. You will stumble over frustration either because things didn't go the way you hoped or because your current circumstances do not live up to those of your past. Don't look back. Stay focused on your mission in Christ. He will take care of the past, present, and future if you keep your mind stayed on Him.

PHILIPPIANS 3:13–14; ISAIAH 43:19;
EPHESIANS 2:10

✦ PRAYER ✦

*Holy Spirit, when my mind wanders away
from Your truth, please speak to my heart
and remind me that the past is the past and
the future is bright. Please give me a glimpse
of what lies ahead so I can press on toward
that higher calling of God in Christ Jesus.*

KEEP CRYING OUT

*S*OMETIMES WHEN YOU stand up for what is right, people around you will call you a fanatic and say you are overreacting. But truth is truth, and you are called to proclaim it. Sometimes when you pursue Jesus with all your heart, all your mind, all your soul, and all your strength, people will say you are too fervent. But fire is fire.

Remember blind Bartimaeus! He needed a touch from Jesus, so instead of remaining silent when the Messiah went by, he cried out to Him. The people around him told him to quiet his mouth, but he cried out all the more. Don't stop crying out for truth. Don't stop crying out for a touch from Jesus. Don't let anyone put out your fire. We love it!

LUKE 10:27; JOHN 14:6; MARK 10:46–52

→ PRAYER ←

I want to burn and shine for You even when people don't understand my love for You. Help me to share Your heart with the people around me so they can know You the way I do and burn and shine with me.

January 20

SET YOUR MIND AND HEART ON JESUS

*A*LWAYS REMEMBER THIS: you are *in* the world but not *of* the world. Set your mind and your heart on Jesus, and He will refresh your soul. Don't look to the right or to the left because that's where the enemy lies in wait. Look for Jesus along the narrow way. Wait on Jesus. Trust in Jesus.

Father gave you the dreams, visions, and desires of your heart, and He will bring them to pass in His way and in His time and in His season. Don't give up now. The enemy is no match for the one who loves Jesus. Take hold of My heart afresh. I won't let you down.

JOHN 17:16–26; HEBREWS 12:2; PSALM 37:4

⟶ PRAYER ⟵

Give me laserlike focus on Your will so that I will not be moved by the distractions that come from the world and from the enemy of my soul. Teach me to trust You and Your timing for the good things You have planned for me.

ASK ME FOR THE WISDOM TO SET BOUNDARIES

*P*EOPLE WILL PUSH you to the point of absolute exhaustion if you let them. They don't mean to, and you don't have to let them. Some people always want more, more, more, and more, and they don't realize you don't have more to give unless you tell them. You need to give out only what We give you to share.

If you don't set boundaries in your life, you will become stressed out and worn out and will eventually burn out. But seclude yourself in My presence, and you will find refreshing and restoration for your weary soul. I have the wisdom you need to set the proper boundaries in your life. Just ask Me.

LUKE 5:15–16; MATTHEW 5:37; MATTHEW 11:28

→ PRAYER ←

My heart is to help people, but I sometimes wear myself out by not asking You first. Remind me to acknowledge You before making a commitment so I don't burn out and end up resenting the people I have a heart to help. Teach me to say no graciously.

January 22

DON'T GET DISCOURAGED WHEN YOU ENCOUNTER RESISTANCE

WHEN YOU FACE opposition in trying to walk through the doorway to Father's promises, don't get frustrated or discouraged. When you meet with resistance, it usually means you're on the right path. There's little resistance on the broad path. The narrow path is full of pressure—the pressure of dying to self to do what's right and the pressure from the enemy to get back on the broad path. I can show you how to find the doorway to Father's promises. Then it's up to you to knock and keep on knocking. Father will surely open the door at the appointed time.

MATTHEW 7:13–14; MATTHEW 16:24;
MATTHEW 7:7

> ✦ PRAYER ✦
>
> *Show me Your paths and help me to walk
> in Your ways. Give me a persevering
> spirit that refuses to draw back in the face
> of opposition to Your will for my life. I
> trust You to lead me and guide me and
> open the right doors at the right time.*

RENEW YOUR MIND

*L*ISTEN TO YOUR self-talk. What are you telling yourself about your circumstances? If you pay close attention, you'll notice it's not the circumstance that has you in a tizzy—it's how you *perceive* the circumstance.

Renew your mind to see things the way I see them. Look through the lens of the Word and you will stop the devil's lies from taking root in your soul. As a man thinketh in his heart, so is he. What are you thinking in your heart? How does that line up with the Word of God? See for yourself.

PROVERBS 23:7; ROMANS 12:2; PHILIPPIANS 4:8

✦ PRAYER ✦

Forgive me for looking at circumstances instead of looking at Your promises, and help me to renew my mind with Your Word. I want my thought life to glorify You. I want to see things the way You do. Please help me today and every day.

January 24

Enter Into My Rest

REST IN ME. Yes, enter into My rest. As you believe that I am a rewarder of those who diligently seek Me, that My Word does not return to Me void but accomplishes that which I sent it to do, and that I am faithful even when you are faithless—when you believe all this in the face of any situation—you will enter My rest, and the peace that surpasses all understanding will flood your heart and soul. There is rest for the weary. And you are in the midst of the One who is inviting you to enter His rest. Will you accept My invitation?

HEBREWS 11:6; ISAIAH 55:11; 2 TIMOTHY 2:13

⤖ PRAYER ⬻

Yes, I accept Your invitation to enter Your rest. Please show me how to shake off the fearful, faithless thoughts that are clouding the truth in my mind. I believe that You are faithful and that Your Word is true. Help me apply it to my life and walk in Your peace.

I AM COMMITTED TO YOU

WHEN I CAME to make My home in your heart, I committed Myself to you fully. I committed My grace and power to you. I committed My kindness and patience to you. I committed My comfort and wisdom to you. I committed My mercy and love to you. I committed all that I am and all that I have to you. I will not break My commitment to you. It is everlasting to everlasting. You and I—we are one. I am always with you. Know this and walk confidently before friend and foe. My favor is upon you.

1 CORINTHIANS 6:19; HEBREWS 13:20–21; HEBREWS 13:5

→ PRAYER ←

Thank You for Your covenant with me. Thank You for Your grace, power, kindness, patience, comfort, wisdom, mercy, love, and favor toward me. Help me walk confidently in the spiritual blessings You have poured out on me.

REJOICE IN GOD!

THERE IS STRENGTH in My joy. When you rejoice in Father, you draw on His wisdom. When you rejoice in Jesus and what He did for you at Calvary, you draw on His unmatchable grace. When you rejoice in Me and who I am for you, you draw on My power to overcome any and every obstacle. You are strengthened in spirit, soul, and body when you rejoice in Us.

You have the opportunity and freedom to rejoice anytime you choose. So lift up your voice and lift up your heart to Me, and I will strengthen you. I want to strengthen you. When you are weak, I am strong.

PSALM 28:7; PHILIPPIANS 4:4;
2 CORINTHIANS 12:10

✦ PRAYER ✦

My heart rejoices in You. I rejoice in Your wisdom, grace, and power. Thank You for empowering me to overcome any and every obstacle that hinders a more intimate relationship with You. Thank You for victory in every area of my life!

MOVE OUT IN FAITH

*Y*OUR CAPACITY TO receive from My Spirit will continue to expand as you move out in faith toward what lies ahead. That requires you to shake some things loose that have held you back, slowed you down, or hindered your progress. You have seen some of these things but have been blind to others.

I will show you what you need to see when you need to see it. When I show you, move out in faith. Get in agreement with Me. Let it go, and don't look back. I want more of you. Embrace more of Me. Welcome the change My Spirit brings. It's good.

HEBREWS 12:1; PSALM 119:18; EPHESIANS 1:18

⇀ PRAYER ↽

Open the eyes of my heart! Help me to see those things I cannot see that are diluting my faith. I want to see the way You see so I can agree with Your heart. I welcome the changes You are making in my life. I yield to You.

January 28

MY HAND IS ALWAYS ON YOU

MY HAND IS always on you. When you go through the fire, My hand is on you. When you walk through the wilderness, My hand is on you. Even in the valley of the shadow of death My hand is on you. On the mountaintop of victory My hand is on you. In the overflow of abundance and in the scarcity of lack My hand is on you. Whether in sorrow or in rejoicing, My hand is on you. Remember this truth in *every* season, good or bad.

I am in control, and I am ordering your steps. So walk in faith knowing that My hand is on you and no one can take you from Me.

ISAIAH 43:2; PSALM 23:4; PHILIPPIANS 4:12–13

⇥ PRAYER ⇤

I am so grateful that You are always with me, no matter what season, test, or trial I walk through! Please give me a greater revelation of Your grace and Your presence in the midst of the hard times. I am content in Your presence.

Go Deeper in My Love

*N*OTHING CAN STOP you from entering the depths of My love except wrong thoughts and beliefs about who I am. I want to take you deeper, but you must see another dimension of My heart to become willing to abandon yourself more fully to Me. The enemy wants you to fear the new level I desire to bring you into. But My perfect love will cast out fear—if you let it. Meditate on My love for you, and follow Me into the secret place, where I can share the depth of My compassion for you. You will never be the same.

1 John 4:18; Psalm 91:1

→ Prayer ←

I want to go deeper with You. Show me where my thoughts and beliefs are out of line with Your truth. Show me Your heart of love and compassion for me. Take me to Your secret place, where I can come to know You better.

January 30

LAY ASIDE EVERY WEIGHT

*L*AY ASIDE EVERY weight that slows you down. You know what some of those weights are. Roll those cares over on Me. They hinder your race. But there are other weights—wounds and bruises— that you don't even remember sustaining. I saw you set your face like flint and plow through in My will. I helped you. I saw the coarse jesting that came against you; the harsh words of disapproval; the broken relationships. Those are weights slowing you down. Yield to Me now. Let Me wash over you and cleanse your heart from the residue of those pains. Let the healing balm of Gilead do its work.

1 PETER 5:7; PSALM 55:22; JEREMIAH 8:21–22

→ PRAYER ←

I refuse to allow the cares of this world or wounds from the past to slow me down any longer, but I need Your grace. Wash over me with Your healing power and help me forgive those who have wronged me. I choose to forgive.

OPEN YOUR SPIRITUAL EYES

OPEN YOUR EYES wide to see what the Word really says. Open your spiritual eyes, and you will see and understand the true meaning of the words I inspired. Let them inspire you. Let them strengthen you. Let them direct you. Open your eyes wide to see what the Word really says—and when you've seen all you think there is to see, turn to Me again. I will open your eyes even wider and pour out wisdom and revelation. I want you to see the depths of Father's love for you. I want you to enter into a new dimension of the mind of Christ. So ask Me to open your eyes.

LUKE 24:45; EPHESIANS 1:17;
1 CORINTHIANS 2:16

→ PRAYER ←

I am determined to open my eyes wide, but I know that only You can help me grasp the revelation in the Word. So I ask You to open my eyes and help me understand the Scriptures. Open my understanding.

February

If you love Me, keep My commandments. I will
pray the Father, and He will give you another
Counselor, that He may be with you forever: the
Spirit of truth, whom the world cannot receive, for
it does not see Him, neither does it know Him. But
you know Him, for He lives with you, and will be
in you.... But the Counselor, the Holy Spirit, whom
the Father will send in My name, will teach you
everything and remind you of all that I told you.

—JOHN 14:15–17, 26

SEEK MY DISCERNMENT

ERCEPTION IS NOT always reality. What you perceive about other people is not always accurate. What other people perceive about you is not always accurate. So stop depending on your perceptions—what you see, what you hear, and what other people tell you—and seek My discernment on matters large and small. Wrong perceptions lead to presumption, and presumption can devastate relationships. Don't allow wrong perceptions to become a snare to you.

1 CORINTHIANS 13:7; PHILIPPIANS 1:9–10;
JOHN 7:24

⇢ PRAYER ⇠

*Please give me discernment and help me to avoid
the sin of presumption in all my ways. Help
me to believe the best and to see people the way
You see them. Show me where I have wrongly
judged another so I will not fall into a snare.*

February 2

ENTER A SEASON OF RECONCILIATION

*R*ECONCILIATION MUST OCCUR before you can see restoration. Something that is not first reconciled cannot be restored. So enter now into a season of reconciliation. Seek out those with whom there is a breach in the spirit. Seek to clear offenses. Offer a hand of peace. Forgive and let go.

I want to do new things in old relationships. I want to heal and restore. So enter into a season of reconciliation and watch My hand move in your life in a mighty way.

2 CORINTHIANS 5:18; PROVERBS 18:19;
MATTHEW 5:23–26

⇾ PRAYER ⇽

I choose to forgive. I choose to reconcile. I choose to live in peace with all people as far as it depends on me. Please lead me and guide me toward reconciliation in Your way, in Your timing, and for Your purposes and glory.

MEDITATE ON WHAT YOU ARE LEARNING

TAKE A MOMENT—TAKE some time—to meditate on the lessons you are learning. I am teaching you new things and reminding you of things you know that have slipped out of focus in the midst of the warfare around you. Consider what I have taught you. Meditate on those truths. Record them on the tablets of your heart. Never forget them. Call them up when you need them. This wisdom will serve you and others around you in the days ahead.

JOHN 14:26; PROVERBS 7:2–3;
1 CORINTHIANS 2:13

⇥ PRAYER ⇤

Put me in remembrance of the teachings of Christ and the words of wisdom You've spoken to my heart. I ask You now for the grace to draw on what You've taught me so that I will walk in Father's ways and glorify my Savior through my words, thoughts, and actions.

February 4

BEWARE OF THE FIRE STARTERS

SOME PEOPLE WILL seek to take advantage of relational difficulties between you and those closest to you: your partners, co-laborers, friends, and family. These people are fire starters—their tongues are set on fire with flames from hell, and they launch fiery darts against you in the name of care and concern. Those who are truly concerned about you and your relationships will seek to *put out* fires—not *start* them. So beware of those with wagging tongues, even when they seem to have your best interest at heart.

PROVERBS 26:20–22; PROVERBS 16:28;
JAMES 3:6 8; MATTHEW 5:9

✦ PRAYER ✦

Help me to close the door to gossip and slander. Help me to discern when someone—knowingly or unknowingly—is trying to set off a fire in my relationships with others. Give me the wisdom to respond rightly and walk in peace with all people.

I HAVE THE SOLUTION

*J*UST TRUST Me with it. Am I not worthy of your trust? Have I not earned it? Do I not deserve it? Just trust Me with it. Whenever you encounter anything you can't handle, just trust Me with it. I see the end from the beginning. I know the way through and the way out. I know the way over and the way under. I have the solution to all your problems. Just trust Me with it. Give it to Me now, and rejoice in My love.

2 SAMUEL 7:28; PSALM 13:5; PSALM 20:7

⊹ PRAYER ⊱

I trust You. I will not be moved from Your heart of love, yet help me to trust You more and more. Help me to rejoice in Your love even in the midst of trials. Speak to my heart during times of trouble, and show me the pathway to peace.

February 6

MY INTENTIONS TOWARD
YOU ARE PERFECT

F YOU REALLY knew how good I am, if you really understood how patient I am, if you really had a revelation of how much I love you, you would realize that My intentions toward you are perfect. I am on your side. I am cheering you on in your race. When you stumble, I am ready to pick you up, dust you off, and heal your heart. I am good. I am patient. I am kind. I love you. If you only knew! Consider these truths because they will set you free to love Me more and to receive more of Me and *from Me.*

PSALM 136:1; PSALM 100:5; PSALM 107:1

→ PRAYER ←

*Wash over me with Your love, and let me taste
and see just how good You really are. Help me
to reject guilt and condemnation when I stumble,
and give me a tender heart that will accept
Your invitation to repentance and forgiveness.*

SEEK MY COUNSEL IN CONFUSING TIMES

*Y*OU CAN GET wise counsel from people in the midst of a complex situation, and you should. Wisdom can come from the experiences of godly men and women. But always remember this: only I know what is best. I have the mind of the Father—in every situation. Don't neglect My counsel in the midst of the confusion. I am your Counselor. So before you act on any counsel from men—even the wisest men—always confirm it with Me. I will lead you into peace.

JOHN 14:26; 1 CORINTHIANS 2:11; ROMANS 9:1

→ PRAYER ←

I am grateful that there is wisdom in the counsel of many, but I recognize that You have all wisdom and that You lead me forth by peace. Help me to always seek Your counsel, Your wisdom, and Your confirmation on all my decisions.

February 8

SPEAK AND THINK ABOUT MY WORDS

*Y*OU CAN PRAY without speaking, and you can see without opening your eyes. But when you move in the realm of the unspoken and the unseen, you may encounter false voices and false visions from the enemy that aim to skew your perspective. Be cautious not to speak about the enemy's plan over your life because the power of life and death are in the tongue. Be careful not to meditate on the vain imaginations he gives you. They move you away from the truth of My heart and into deception. Speak and think about My words.

1 JOHN 4:1; PROVERBS 18:21; 2 CORINTHIANS 10:5

✦ PRAYER ✦

Set a guard over my eyes, my ears, and my mouth. Give me the diligence to guard my heart because out of it flow the issues of life. Help me to recognize the vain imaginations and false voices that seek to betray Your truth. Help me to take every thought captive that is not of You.

LEARN TO DISCERN YOUR
TIMES AND SEASONS

EASONS CHANGE, but I never do. Time goes on, but I know the end from the beginning. I see all your days. I see all your times. I see all your seasons. I see all your peaks and all your valleys. Seasons come and go. You will pass through them one at a time, one after another—and always in My perfect timing.

Know this: I am orchestrating your times and your seasons. I am ordering your steps, and My path is perfect. Learn to discern your times and seasons. Don't lag behind. Don't get ahead. Walk with Me, and we will do great and awesome things together.

ECCLESIASTES 3:1; ISAIAH 46:10; PSALM 37:23

→ PRAYER ←

Thank You that You never change. Thank You that You are with me through all my times and seasons. Give me a discerning heart, and don't let me fall behind but hold my hand and guide me along Your paths for the glory of Christ.

February 10

BLESSED ARE THE PEACEMAKERS

When you see fires, put them out. I have called you to be a peacemaker. The enemy uses the tongue of man to start fires that originate in hell. Such fires seek to divide, distress, and disgust the brethren. But as for you, put out the fires with words of love. Don't engage in the strife; squash it with words of faith. I will use your words of faith and love to convict the offenders so they will repent, turn their hearts toward Me, and speak of good things. Blessed are the peacemakers.

JAMES 3:6; PROVERBS 26:20; MATTHEW 5:9

→ PRAYER ←

*Set a guard over my mouth and help me
to speak words that are pleasing to You.
Give me wisdom to discern the beginnings
of strife so that I do not participate in the
enemy's plan, and help me to be a maker
and maintainer of peace in every situation.*

You Won't Miss Your Destiny

Stay in close fellowship with Me, and I will show you the next step in My plan for you. It will be clear. Don't worry; you won't miss your destiny in the midst of the chaos that sometimes surrounds you. The promises Father has made to you will come to pass if you act in faith. Press in and refuse to shrink back in the face of opposition from man and beast.

No one can steal your destiny. No one can interfere with the fulfillment of My will in your life but you. Stick close to Me. I will lead you where I want you to go.

John 16:13; John 10:28; 1 Corinthians 2:10

✦ Prayer ✦

Thank You for always getting my attention when my heart begins to stray from You. Strengthen my spirit to press into Father's good plan, and help me to overcome the obstacles the enemy puts in my path to hinder my progress in Your will.

February 12

I WILL REORDER YOUR STEPS

*E*VERYONE MAKES MISTAKES. Don't dwell on yours! Meditate on Me, and I will reorder your steps, restore what was lost, and reveal where you will go and what you will do next. I'm that good. I'm that powerful. Your decisions will be informed by My wisdom as you learn to recognize My ways in this new season. You are in a different place today than you were a year ago. But My faithfulness to you is constant. Believe that.

PSALM 37:23; DEUTERONOMY 30:3;
1 CORINTHIANS 1:9

→ PRAYER ←

Thank You for Your goodness. Thank You
for Your power. Thank You for Your wisdom.
Thank You for Your restoration and rev-
elation in my life. Thank You for teaching
me Your ways and showing me Your
paths. Thank You for Your faithfulness.

PRAY WITH ME

WHEN YOU PRAY with Me—when you yield yourself to Me by praying in the Spirit—you are speaking mysteries. You are praying the perfect prayer. You are in My will. So when you don't know how to pray as you ought—and even when you think you know what to pray—let Me help you. Yield to Me in prayer. Partner with Me in prayer, and expect Father to deliver supernatural answers that you aren't expecting.

EPHESIANS 6:18; 1 CORINTHIANS 14:2;
ROMANS 8:26

→ PRAYER ←

I don't always know what to pray or how to pray, but You do. Help me to yield to You in prayer. Stir my spirit to pray when You want to pray. Show me whom and what to pray for. Pray with me and through me for Father's perfect will to come to pass.

DISCOVER THE POWER OF UNITY

I WANT YOU TO grasp the concept of unity at a deeper level. It will be important as I take you to the next place I want you to go. You understand the destructive power of strife, but let Me reveal to you now the exponential power of unity.

Look past your differences with other believers, and seek to find synergies that can advance the kingdom. This will not only increase the anointing on your life but also bear much fruit—eternal fruit—for the kingdom. Start today.

PSALM 133:1; JOHN 17:23; EPHESIANS 4:1;
COLOSSIANS 3:14

→ PRAYER ←

Give me a revelation of unity—a deep revelation of how vital unity is—that will change my paradigm. Let me see what You see and feel what You feel about strife so that I will avoid it at every turn. Give me the grace of humility and help me to walk in unity.

WATCH YOUR WORDS

*B*E CAUTIOUS NOT to engage in idle conversations, for you will give account of every idle word on the Day of Judgment. Be aware of the impact of the words you speak to bring life or death into situations and souls. Be vigilant about blessing and not cursing. For you reap what you sow, and you eat the words of your mouth. Tend to the fountain in your heart so it puts forth fresh water that refreshes the hearers and builds faith in their souls.

MATTHEW 12:36; PROVERBS 18:21; ROMANS 12:14

✦ PRAYER ✦

Help me to see clearly the power of life and death in my words so that I will speak only life over myself and others. I don't want to speak idle words. I don't want to speak harmful words. Help me avoid corrupt communication, and let my speech edify others.

February 16

Approach the Day With Gladness

Count your blessings. Boast in Jesus. Approach the day with gladness in your heart. Let the joy of the Lord consume you. The people and situations you face from day to day can indeed be troublesome, but a glad and grateful heart that rejoices in its salvation will sustain and strengthen you through the wind, the rain, the fire, and the storm. Boast in Jesus and bless His name. Worthy is the Lamb.

Philippians 4:4; James 1:2–4; Psalm 13:5

→ Prayer ←

I bless the name of Jesus! I choose to rejoice this day in my salvation! Worthy is the Lamb of God who took away my sin. No matter what situations I face—no matter what trials come my way—I commit to rejoicing in Almighty God. He is worthy!

Don't Give Up on Your Dreams

*Y*ou may know My will and My ways, but Father's timing is of vital importance. So don't allow the enemy to deceive you. Don't give up on your God-given dreams. Don't abandon the desires of your heart. Don't stop interceding for the people who weigh on your soul and the circumstances that concern you.

Jesus is the author and finisher of your faith, and all Father's promises are yes and amen. So hold tight and hang on. Your dreams will come to pass at the perfect time. I assure you the time is coming.

Habakkuk 2:3; Ecclesiastes 3:1;
2 Corinthians 1:20; Galatians 6:9

✦ Prayer ✦

*Holy Spirit, help me to recognize Father's timing
so that I don't rush ahead of His will. Help
me not grow weary in doing good so that I can
reap in due season. Help me to hold on to the
great and precious promises He has given me.*

February 18

RECEIVE THE FEAR OF THE LORD

*A*S THE WORLD continues to grow darker, let your heart receive the fear of the Lord, and it will be a fountain of life to you. The fear of the Lord is the beginning of wisdom and will lead you out of temptation's grip and help you work out your own salvation with fear and trembling. In the fear of the Lord there is strong confidence, and Father's mercy shall be with you even when you stumble and fall. I want to release the fear of the Lord into your heart and teach you to acknowledge Me in all your ways.

PROVERBS 1:7; PROVERBS 14:26; JOB 28:28

✦ PRAYER ✦

Release the fear of the Lord into my heart. Help me work out my salvation with fear and trembling. I refuse to compromise with the spirit of the world or bow to the will of man. I choose to be a friend of God and walk in Your statutes.

Embrace the Refiner's Fire

$\mathcal{M}$Y REFINING FIRE is hot, but it will not burn you. Embrace the heat. Embrace the fire. Embrace the discomfort. My purifying fire is purging your soul of impurities that hinder love. This fire is burning away that which is keeping you from My absolute best for your life. The heat is drawing you closer to Me as you seek to understand what is happening in your soul. You don't need to have all the answers. Just know that I am working in your soul and in your spirit, and My work is always good.

1 PETER 1:7; PSALM 66:10–12; ISAIAH 48:10

✦ PRAYER ✦

Purify my heart, O God. Purify my soul. I trust in You. You will never harm me. You will never leave me. Let Your love burn through everything that is slowing me down as I run this race. I yield to Your Spirit even in the fire.

YOU HAVE ALL YOU NEED

I KNOW ALL THINGS, and I see all things, and I understand all things. Trusting Me means you don't need to know all things and see all things and understand all things. You have *Me*. You have all you need in Christ.

Seek to know Me the way I know you. Seek to know Father. Seek to know Christ. As you grow in relationship with Us, knowing Us will be enough for you. You won't search for answers; you'll search for Me, and I will give you the answers you need when you need them.

PROVERBS 3:5; PSALM 46:10; DEUTERONOMY 4:29

✦ PRAYER ✦

You love those who love You, and if I seek You diligently, I will find You. Let me be content in knowing Your heart. Help me to avoid the reasoning and questionings that distract me from Your love. I choose to trust You always in all things.

ASK FOR A DISCERNING SPIRIT

I WANT YOU TO learn to discern My presence and the opposition to My will. I want to increase the gift of discerning of spirits in your life. This gift is vital to your ability to fulfill your calling.

Where My Spirit is, there is liberty, peace, joy, and love. Where strife exists, there is confusion and every evil work. The contrast seems clear, but many times only a discerning spirit will perceive what is operating behind the scenes. Ask Me for a discerning spirit, and I will give it to you.

PHILIPPIANS 1:9–10; HEBREWS 4:12; JAMES 3:16

✦ PRAYER ✦

Sharpen my discernment so that I may know and recognize what is going on in the spirit realm. I want to know Your presence in a greater way. I want to see the traps the enemy has erected to snare my soul. Give me a discerning spirit that sees as You see.

February 22

REFOCUS YOUR MIND

I'VE MADE YOU holy even as I am holy. When you think, speak, and act in a way that violates My holiness, you have stopped looking at Jesus. He still abides in you because He will never leave you or forsake you, but you have taken your eyes off Him. You have focused on the circumstances the enemy is showing you, continued to think about the frustrations, and forgotten the power that dwells in you to resist the temptations of your flesh. Refocus your mind on My holiness, and you will once again experience the blessing of living and moving and having your being in Jesus.

1 Peter 1:16; Hebrews 13:5; Acts 17:28

→ PRAYER ←

Thank You for Your purifying power at work in my life. Help me to stay focused on Jesus. I refuse to meditate on the negative things the enemy of my soul puts before me. Help me to recognize the devil's lies at the onset and stay focused on Your truth.

Don't Try to Be Like Anyone Else

*D*on't try to be like anyone else. I love you just the way Father created you. When you compare yourself to others, you will always find something to be proud about and something to feel bad about. Before you were formed in your mother's womb, I knew you. I loved you—and I liked you. I enjoy your uniqueness, and I want you to appreciate yourself as My creation. I am changing you from glory to glory, but I love you just as you are in Christ.

Ephesians 2:10; 2 Corinthians 10:12;
Jeremiah 1:5

→ Prayer ←

Thank You for loving me. Thank You for encouraging me to be everything Father created me to be. Please help me not to compare myself to others so that I don't discourage my soul or puff myself up. Help me see myself the way You see me.

TODAY IS A NEW DAY

ODAY IS A new day. Leave yesterday's worries behind, reject tomorrow's anxieties, and believe that I will lead you and guide you through this day. Believe that I will give you the grace you need because I am your grace. Believe that I will give you the wisdom you need because I am your wisdom. Believe that I will give you the peace you need because I am your peace. I am your standby, waiting to provide whatever you need today and every day.

PHILIPPIANS 3:13–14; MATTHEW 6:25;
JOHN 14:26

→ PRAYER ←

Help me to walk by faith—to live by faith—one day at a time, recognizing that You are walking with me and will help Me. When I begin to worry or stress, remind me that You are with me, and allow me to feel Your sweet presence.

LET ME LEAD YOU INTO JESUS'S REST

WHEN YOU AREN'T resting in Christ, My heart aches for you. Jesus has invited you to enter His rest, and I will lead you there as you offer up prayer and supplication with thanksgiving. Let Me help you to make your requests known to Father. Jesus is ever making intercession for you at the right hand of Father. I am your intercessor here on the earth. I want to help you pray when you don't know how to yield to My heart. Pray with Me, and enter into Christ's rest now.

HEBREWS 4:3; PHILIPPIANS 4:6–7; ROMANS 8:34

✦ PRAYER ✦

Some days are so stressful. Please help me enter into Christ's rest—and walk in that rest—all day, every day. Thank You for helping me to cast my cares on the Lord. Thank You for leading me and guiding me to a place where peace dwells.

February 26

NEVER LET GO OF GOD'S PROMISE

I KNOW YOU'VE BEEN waiting for a long time to see that prayer answered. But don't let go of Father's promise. When you stand on the Word of God, you will not stumble. When you confess My will in the face of an opposite reality, it strengthens your faith. When you commit to waiting to see My glory manifest in your circumstances, you develop the patience that holds up your faith and allows you to inherit the promises you have long hoped to see manifest. Now is the time to press in harder. I am for you, not against you. And if I am for you, who can be against you?

HEBREWS 6:12; ISAIAH 40:8; ROMANS 8:31

→ PRAYER ←

I get tired of waiting to see answers to prayer. I get disappointed and impatient. Help me to stand in faith, knowing that the Word of God will work in my life if I continue to press into the promise with persistence. Give me a steadfast spirit.

GRASP THE BENEFITS OF THIS REVELATION

*J*OSHUA AND DAVID had something in common, and if you grasp a significant revelation they had, it will change your mind, change your speech, change your actions, build your faith, tear down strongholds, ease your fears, give you strength, offer you direction, and totally transform your life. I want to share this simple revelation with you today and help you practice it: meditate on the Word day and night. Will you go on this journey to renewing your mind with Me?

JOSHUA 1:8; PSALM 19:14; PSALM 1:2

⇢ PRAYER ⇠

*David and Joshua left such strong examples of
walking in Your statutes. Give me the same grace
of obedience that was on them as they pursued
Your will. Thank You for renewing my mind
as I meditate on Your Word day and night.*

February 28

DON'T FOCUS ON THE ENEMY

I SEE YOUR ENEMY rising up against you, but that doesn't move Me. The enemy of your faith is always working to distract you from My truth and from our fellowship together. Don't let him succeed! When you focus too much on what the enemy is doing in your life, you disturb your inner peace and open the door to fear, doubt, and unbelief in Father's promises to you.

See your enemy, but don't focus on him. Take authority over his operations in the name of Jesus. Discern the attack, but deal with it and move on in Jesus. The victory belongs to you.

DEUTERONOMY 28:7; LUKE 10:19; 1 PETER 5:9

✦ PRAYER ✦

No foe can withstand Your power. Every knee must bow and every tongue confess that Jesus is Lord. Therefore I will not allow the enemy to sway me from Your truth. Help me to resist him, standing firm in the faith, when he comes to distract me.

JESUS IS YOUR HEALER

*F*ATHER IS *JEHOVAH Rapha.* Jesus is your healer. By His stripes, you are healed. Think about those words. Meditate on them. Tell others about the healing power in the atonement. Faith comes by hearing the Word of God, and My word to you is "healing"—healing for your body when you are sick, healing for your soul when you are hurt, healing for your relationships when they are broken. I am revealing Christ to you as your healer. Receive the fullness of your salvation.

EXODUS 15:26; ISAIAH 53:5; 1 PETER 2:24

✦ PRAYER ✦

Thank You for a revelation of the atonement. As I am faithful to meditate on the Word of God for healing, release Your power into my body, my mind, and my life to heal all those things that need healing and restoration. Help me to walk in divine health.

March

Nevertheless I tell you the truth: It is expedient for you that I go away. For if I do not go away, the Counselor will not come to you. But if I go, I will send Him to you. When He comes, He will convict the world of sin and of righteousness and of judgment: of sin, because they do not believe in Me; of righteousness, because I am going to My Father, and you will see Me no more; and of judgment, because the ruler of this world stands condemned.

—JOHN 16:7–11

Rise Up in My Power

*R*ise up in My power and face the day's challenges head-on. Don't shrink back, look back, or slide back. Realize that you are blessed with every spiritual blessing in heavenly places and that you can do all things through Christ who gives you strength. Draw on the blessings by thanking Me for them. Draw on the strength by taking a step forward in faith. Rise up in My power, and I will go before you and make a way where there is no way. I won't let you down.

Ephesians 1:3; Philippians 4:13;
2 Samuel 22:33

→ Prayer ←

*Thank You that Your power dwells in me
and makes me ready to meet every challenge that comes my way. I will move forward in Your strength, not my own, knowing
that it empowers me to do everything I
need to do. Thank You for Your power!*

March 2

I Will Help You Reach Your Destiny

I WILL BRING PEOPLE across your path to help you accomplish what I have called you to do. I will help you make the connections—and connect the dots. Yes, I will direct your steps toward the people, places, and things you need to reach your destiny in Christ. That is My part and My joy. Your part is to ask Me, to seek Me, to hear Me, and to follow and obey Me. We are in this together. I will do My part. You must do your part.

PSALM 119:133; PROVERBS 2:1–5; JOHN 14:23

❖ PRAYER ❖

Thank You for divine connections. I will expect them. Help me to discern Your leading. Help me to recognize the people You've called to work with me to accomplish Your will. Give me an ear to hear what Your Spirit is saying every step of the way.

PURSUE PURITY AND HOLINESS

*F*EW UNDERSTAND My holiness. I am pure. Even My words are purified seven times. I am pure in My motives toward you. I want the best for you, though I know it doesn't always feel or look like the best.

I am making you holy even as I am holy. I am transforming you into the image of Christ, from glory to glory and from faith to faith. Embrace My holiness. Pursue My purity, and you will rest in My love in a greater way than you ever thought possible.

PSALM 12:6; 2 CORINTHIANS 3:18; ROMANS 12:1; 1 TIMOTHY 4:12

→ PRAYER ←

I know You want the best for me, and I thank You. Help me yield to Your sanctifying power in my life. I desire to be holy even as You are holy. Purge my soul from anything that is not pleasing to You so that I will love You with all my heart.

March 4

TEAR DOWN YOUR IDOLS

I'M CALLING YOU to tear down the idols in your life. Moses did it. Hezekiah did it. Josiah did it. I moved on their hearts to destroy the idols from their midst, and when they obeyed Me, revival broke out before them.

When you heed My voice and tear down the idols in your heart, you will experience a personal revival that will take you to the deeper place in Christ that you have longed for but could not reach. Tear down anything that distracts your heart from My love.

1 JOHN 5:21; 1 CORINTHIANS 10:14; LUKE 9:23

✦ PRAYER ✦

Show me where I have erected idols in my life so that I may tear them down and destroy them. I desire to exalt God and God alone. I desire a personal awakening. Stir my spirit and give me the strength to rid my life of anything that stands between us.

FOLLOW ME

*I*KNOW THE WAY to your strong tower. I will lead you to the place of peace and protection in the midst of the storm, so follow Me. I will lead you and guide you into truth and into safety. Father will keep you in the shadow of His wings, and Jesus will lead you into triumph.

Follow Me as I exalt Christ in your heart and in your life. We are on your side. No foe can withstand Our power. Just focus on Us and Our love for you. You cannot fail.

PROVERBS 18:10; PSALM 91; PSALM 17:8

→ PRAYER ←

You are my strong tower. You are my peace. You are my shelter in the midst of the storm. I thank You for Your protection, Your victory, Your peace, and Your love. Help me to stay focused on Your truth, and give me an enduring spirit.

March 6

DON'T BE A PEOPLE PLEASER

*D*ON'T BE A people pleaser or make decisions based on the backlash you expect from others who don't get what they want from you. People will pull you right out of Father's will into their own will if you let them. There's a difference between walking in love and being walked on. Politely refuse that which you know is not My will, no matter who is pressuring you. Ask Me what I would have you do; obey and then let it go. Leave the people to Father. Keep your head up and move forward with what Father told you to do.

COLOSSIANS 3:24; EPHESIANS 5:17; ACTS 5:29

→ PRAYER ←

I don't want to be a people pleaser. I want to be a God pleaser. Help me avoid the temptation to submit to the will of man when You have called me to do something else. Help me to choose the God things over the good things man proposes.

NO FOE CAN WITHSTAND YOU

*N*o foe can withstand My power. My enemies tremble at the name of Jesus. Your spiritual enemies are My enemies, and My power dwells in you. Therefore, no foe can withstand you as you walk in My power and exercise your authority in Christ.

Open your heart now and think on these truths, and I will renew your vision. I will remove the blinders that allow your foes to appear victorious in your sight. You will rise up in My power with your enemies under your feet.

JAMES 2:19; MARK 16:17; MATTHEW 22:44

→ PRAYER ←

Thank You, Jesus, for the victory You won at Calvary. Give me a revelation of my authority in You and the power that dwells within me. Help me to wield the sword of the Spirit against the spiritual enemies that contend with Your will.

March 8

YOUR VICTORY IS GUARANTEED

*Y*ES, IT'S TRUE that the enemy is waiting for his next best opportunity to throw a fiery dart your way. It's true that the devil roams about like a roaring lion seeking someone whom he may devour. But there are greater truths you should focus on—truths that assure you victory: You are more than a conqueror in Christ Jesus. Greater is He that is in you than he that is in the world. No weapon formed against you will prosper.

Condemn those demonic tongues that rise up against you in your imagination, and cast them under your feet with the Word of God. You are victorious!

EPHESIANS 6:10–16; ROMANS 8:37; 1 JOHN 4:4; ISAIAH 54:17

✦ PRAYER ✦

Thank You for equipping me with Your armor to battle against those forces that battle against me. I put on the whole armor of God right now, and I know that when I move out at Your prompting, You will lead me into victory in Christ every time!

COMPREHEND AND SHARE MY LOVE

*J*ESUS ONCE SAID, "Blessed are the pure in heart, for they shall see God." Purity is vital in this hour. Deception has crept into the body of Christ through insecurities, rejections, and pride as well as through unhealed hurts and wounds inflicted by man and inspired by the wicked one. All these things cause identity problems among My people.

I want to pour out a revelation of the pure love I have for you so that you will become even more deeply rooted and grounded in Jesus and will be able to share My love with others who struggle with identity problems. Know who you really are— and then teach others.

MATTHEW 5:8; EPHESIANS 3:17; COLOSSIANS 2:10

→ PRAYER ←

I want to comprehend how wide, long, high, and deep Christ's love is for me. Help me to grasp it not just by faith but by experiences I can share with others. Root me and ground me even deeper in the love of Christ. Make me a living epistle of Your love.

March 10

LET NO CORRUPT COMMUNICATION COME OUT OF YOUR MOUTH

*W*HAT YOU DON'T see with your own eyes, don't give witness to with your mouth. Don't repeat anything you will not sign your name to. Whoever gossips *to* you will gossip *about* you. And remember, Jesus is watching—and listening—so let no corrupt communication come out of your mouth.

Speak only those things that will build up your brothers and sisters. Don't spread strife. Don't reveal secrets. Avoid foolish and stupid arguments. Now is the time for unity to arise in the body of Christ, and it begins with each individual member. It begins with you. Love conquers all.

JAMES 4:11; EPHESIANS 4:29; 2 TIMOTHY 2:23

→ PRAYER ←

Help me to remember that You hear every word I speak. Help me to avoid silly arguments over things that don't really matter. Help me to say what You would say and nothing more. Season my speech with salt and grace. Heal my tongue.

LOVE WHAT GOD LOVES

ATHER ALWAYS HAS something bigger and better in mind if you will walk toward what He loves, even if that means walking away from what you think *you* love. Here's a promise: you'll discover that you love what *He* loves far more than you loved what you walked away from. So love what He loves and hate what He hates, and you will find yourself in the center of His will with His promises fulfilled. You can't possibly imagine the good things He has planned for you—and you don't have to. Only believe they will come to pass.

PSALM 97:10; EPHESIANS 3:20;
1 CORINTHIANS 2:9

✦ PRAYER ✦

Give me prophetic perspective so that I will see the way You do. I commit to following You wherever You lead me no matter what You lead me away from. I want to walk in Your perfect will and see Your promises come to pass. Guide me.

March 12

Love God With All You Are

*Y*ou love Jesus because He first loved you. Decide to love Us with all your heart, all your soul, all your mind, and all your strength. Refuse to let the enemy paint a picture of Father as angry and mean, ready to club you with a mallet when you make a mistake. Reject anything that hinders love!

Ask Me this morning for an anointing to love Us. You will be amazed at the results of this petition if you lift it up to heaven consistently and are open to receive more from Us.

1 John 4:19; Matthew 22:37;
1 Corinthians 13:4–8

✦ Prayer ✦

I want to love You with everything in me. Holy Spirit, show me again Father's heart. Help me to receive Your love so that I can pour it out on You. Answer my heart's cry by giving me an anointing to love You more and more.

ALL IS NOT LOST

*A*LL IS NOT lost. I know it may look as if all is lost, as if you have to start over again. But don't buy into the enemy's drama and hype. Don't be fooled by what you see. As long as you have Jesus, all is not lost. And you *have* Jesus!

If the devil has trespassed, he will have to repay what he stole from you. So don't continue to focus on what he is doing. Focus on what God has done and what He wants to do. He is your deliverer. He is your restorer. He is your peace. He is with you. All is not lost.

2 CORINTHIANS 5:7; JOEL 2:25; 1 PETER 5:10

✦ PRAYER ✦

*Help me to walk by faith and not by sight. What
I see around me often looks like loss, but I know
You are a God of restoration. I choose this day
to keep my eyes on Your power, Your glory, and
Your grace. I trust You to restore all that was lost.*

Don't Give Up Now!

*Y*OUR GOD-GIVEN DREAMS can come true, but you have to pursue the God who gave you the dreams. You also have to take Spirit-led action in faith toward your godly goals. Yes, you'll meet with spiritual warfare and natural stumbling blocks and be tempted to give up. But don't give up! Don't give in. If you seek first the kingdom of God and My will for your life, you will see your dreams manifest in Father's timing. Just keep pressing in! I am with you!

MATTHEW 6:33; PSALM 37:4; MATTHEW 11:12

✦ PRAYER ✦

You are the Dream Giver. You are the One who empowers me to press into the dreams You have for me. Thank You that as I continue seeking Your face and pressing into Your kingdom with holy determination, You will make those dreams reality for Your glory.

Make Room for Your Gift

Your gift will make room for you. But you have to make room for your gift. In other words, prepare for God to use you in this hour. Yield to My Spirit as I work with you to root out issues in your soul that may be holding you back from your destiny. Equip yourself with materials, study to show yourself approved, and fellowship with Me more—and still more. Talk to Me throughout the day. Your gift will make room for you. But you have to make room for your gift.

Proverbs 18:16; 2 Timothy 2:15;
Galatians 5:25

✦ Prayer ✦

Thank You for the gifts You've given me and the plans You have to use those gifts for Your purposes. Help me to prepare to walk in Your will. Help me to remove from my life the distractions that get in the way of what You want to do.

March 16

ASK ME FOR MY PERSPECTIVE

*I*F WHAT YOU see around you isn't changing, consider the possibility that it's time to change the way you look at things. Ask Me for My perspective on the people, places, and things around you. You will be surprised at the revelation you receive if you really press in—if you really wait on Me. Father's ways are higher than your ways, and His thoughts are higher than your thoughts. So wait on Me, and you will mount up with wings as eagles and gain the prophetic perspective you seek.

ISAIAH 55:9; ISAIAH 40:31; ROMANS 12:2

→ PRAYER ←

Holy Spirit, I need Your perspective. Please open my eyes and show me what I'm missing. Give me a glimpse of what You see in the spirit. Share Your thoughts with me about what I need to change. I will wait on You until You show me.

Pray for Those You've Offended

*Y*OU CAN'T MAKE someone forgive you for a mistake you've made. But refusal on the part of another to offer forgiveness isn't a license for you to get bitter. Pray for those you've offended because Father commands them to forgive. Pray for them to forgive you—not for your sake but for theirs.

When people have unforgiveness in their hearts toward you, it may hurt you—but it is much more harmful to their souls. So ask Me to heal their hearts as well as healing yours from the hurt. Reconciliation may or may not come, but either way you can walk rightly.

MATTHEW 5:23–24; ROMANS 12:20; LUKE 6:27

→ PRAYER ←

I pray right now for those whom I've harmed in any way—whether I know I've harmed them or not—and ask You to help them forgive me. Please show me if there is a kind act I can perform on their behalf, and help me not to take offense if they refuse to forgive me.

LET ME HELP YOU AVOID BURNOUT

*B*OUNDARIES ARE VITAL to your spiritual health. Don't allow people to pull you into things Father has not called you to—or make you feel guilty because you won't participate or won't minister to their needs when I have not given you the green light to get involved. If you don't set up godly boundaries, you'll face burnout and flow in resentment.

Let Me lead you and guide you. I know you have a big heart to help people, but everyone will benefit if you wait to let Me show you what to do and when to do it. If people get angry or upset about it, put them in My hands. I will minister to them. You obey Me.

GALATIANS 6:5; JAMES 1:5; LUKE 5:15–16

→ PRAYER ←

You're right. I want to help, but there are only so many hours in the day. Help me to be slow to respond when someone asks me to do something. Help me to wait on Your leading to get involved. I know You want my best as well as theirs. I trust You

DON'T LET THE ENEMY STOP YOU

*D*ON'T GIVE UP. Part of the enemy's strategy is to bring circumstances into your life and set up imaginations in your mind that cause you to get off your post. When the onslaught comes, you feel as if you just want to quit. But that's when you need to stand and withstand. Father is able to help you stand!

Don't give the enemy the satisfaction of stopping you or slowing you down—even if he knocks you down through a stumbling block of temptation. Get right back up and run hard after Father's will for your life. I am with you. You can do this!

2 CHRONICLES 15:7; GALATIANS 6:9; JOSHUA 1:9

→ PRAYER ←

When I feel like giving up, help me to refocus on the vision You have given me. Show me the big picture. When I fall down, help me to get back up again. I want to run this race and walk worthily. I want to fulfill everything You've called me to do. Help me.

March 20

CRY OUT TO YOUR DELIVERER

*J*ESUS IS YOUR deliverer. When you feel anything trying to hold you back, press you down, or shake you up, cry out to your deliverer and watch Jesus work all things together for good in your life as you continue walking in His Word.

My power is available to set you free from anything and everything that stands in the way of Father's perfect will in your life. Father resists the proud and gives grace to the humble, so humble yourself and receive My help. That's what I'm here for. I am your helper.

PSALM 18:2; ROMANS 8:28; JAMES 4:6

⇒ PRAYER ⇐

I come boldly to Your throne of grace with a humble heart. I need Your help. I need Your deliverance in my life. The pressures are real, and sometimes they weigh me down. Deliver me, or give me the grace to walk rightly in spite of them.

WAIT FOR MY STRATEGY

*Y*OU OFTEN FEEL an urgency to respond when a situation arises—to put out a burning flame before it becomes a raging fire. I understand why. But what would happen if you slowed down and waited on Me to show you a strategy to put out the burning flame? Many times I am already working in the background to put the fire out. If you wait on Me instead of taking action, you'll discover that the fire seems to go out on its own.

Let Me do My work. When I need you to do something, I'll tell you. Pray first. I'll guide you, and we'll make sure the fire gets put out.

JAMES 1:19; PSALM 37:7–9; JAMES 5:8

→ PRAYER ←

Help me wait on You. Give me wisdom and understanding to know how You want me to move—or not move—in every situation. I don't want to move in my wisdom; I want to move in Your wisdom and Your timing. I commit to waiting on You.

March 22

LET PATIENCE HAVE ITS PERFECT WORK

THE PRESSURE, THE trials, and the tribulations you face produce Christ's character in you. Remember that. Keep your cool. Focus on your Father, who loves you, and know that He won't let more come at you or on you than you can bear.

I am here to help you bear the pressure, trials, and tribulations. Put them into perspective. Everything you experience on Earth is temporary, and the trying of your faith produces patience. Let patience have its perfect work so you will be mature in Christ, lacking nothing.

ROMANS 5:3–4; JAMES 1:2–4; JAMES 1:12;
ROMANS 12:12

→ PRAYER ←

I want to be more like Jesus. I know becoming like Him means I will encounter trials that will result in His character being formed in me. Help me not to resist Your work in my life but to rejoice in it. Help me to rejoice in my sufferings, knowing that suffering produces endurance. I need You.

PRAY FOR THOSE WHO HURT YOU

*T*HE DEVIL OFTEN uses people who are close to you to launch fiery darts. Sometimes they get especially angry when you won't give them *what* they want *when* they want it. Other times they speak word curses over your life without realizing what they are doing. Still other times they blame you for their own shortcomings.

Pray for those who fire the darts, get godly counsel, and keep up your shield of faith. Father will work out each situation, and if a relationship you are having difficulty with is truly God-ordained, the test will make it stronger in the end.

ROMANS 12:14; MATTHEW 18:15–17; 1 PETER 4:8

→ PRAYER ←

It's hurtful when people close to me turn against me. Help me to walk in love with those who aren't walking in love with me. Help me to demonstrate the love of Christ, and let that love melt their hearts. Help me to bless and not curse. I choose love.

March 24

STAY TRUE TO THE VISION

SOMETIMES YOU HAVE to make the hard calls. Sometimes you have to take a tough stand. Sometimes you have to disappoint those close to you. Sometimes you have to suffer in flesh and soul to follow Me. But you must make a determination in your heart not to let anyone sway you from the vision you know Father has given you.

Many will come to pull you away from your destiny. They will come with distractions, threats, and even false prophecy. Don't stop building what Father has called you to build. Be a good and faithful servant. I know it's hard on the soul, but the eternal rewards await.

MATTHEW 10:38; LUKE 9:23; NEHEMIAH 6:1–16

✦ PRAYER ✦

I choose to die to self and let Christ live in me—even if the people around me don't share my vision. But I ask You to help my family and friends understand why I choose to follow You and do Your work. Protect me from the enemies who try to stop me.

FORGIVENESS IS A WEAPON

ORGIVENESS IS NOT listed in the Ephesians 6 armor set, but make no mistake—you must be quick to forgive those the enemy uses against you. If you are not quick to forgive—if you hold on to offenses large or small—you put yourself in danger of becoming like the spirits that you so hate. Learning to move in the opposite spirit is one of your safeguards against the deception of unforgiveness. If bitterness is a root that defiles, forgiveness is a stance that purifies.

Forgiveness is a weapon in your spiritual war chest. The enemy has no answer for forgiveness. Why do you think Jesus taught us to forgive daily?

MATTHEW 18:21–22; MATTHEW 6:14;
EPHESIANS 4:31–32

→ PRAYER ←

Thank You for revealing forgiveness as a weapon of warfare. Help me to use this mighty weapon to pull down the strongholds in my soul that are contrary to Your love. I will not hold ought against anyone. I choose to forgive today and every day.

March 26

CHANGE YOUR PERSPECTIVE ABOUT SPIRITUAL ATTACKS

So often when you are in the midst of spiritual warfare, when the enemy is harassing you, I hear you say three words that trouble Me: "I'm under attack." Listen carefully to My words and change your perspective. You are not under attack; the attack is under *you*! The enemy is under your feet, and you are seated over him in heavenly places in Christ Jesus.

Change your perspective! Yes, the enemy is doing his job, but that won't stop you from doing yours. Determine that Father's will shall be done and any enemy that stands in the way of your heavenly assignment must bow in the name of Jesus.

LUKE 20:42–43; EPHESIANS 2:6; ROMANS 14:11

→ PRAYER ←

I declare that I am more than a conqueror in Christ. Help me to speak and act as though I believe this truth when I face enemy attacks. Give me a greater revelation of Your power and the authority Jesus delegated to me as His representative on Earth.

Believe for My Best

Man says, "When it rains, it pours." But We can redeem that worldly cliché for Father's glory. When bad things happen, instead of expecting more bad things to follow, expect My grace to rain down on you—to pour down over you. That's faith. Instead of thinking the worst—instead of letting fear creep in—believe for My protection, deliverance, wisdom, healing, or whatever else you need to pour out as a blessing from heaven. Believe for the overflow of My presence to help you through whatever obstacle or circumstance the enemy has set in your path.

Psalm 112:7; Romans 15:13; Psalm 28:7

→ Prayer ←

I expect good things to happen, even when it looks as if bad things are happening instead. I know You want to and are able to work all things together for good. Help me stand strong in faith even in the face of fearful news. Help me remain hopeful despite hopeless circumstances.

WALK THROUGH THE DOORS GOD OPENS

SOMETIMES THERE'S A demonic gatekeeper standing between you and what God has called you to do. The gatekeeper thinks he has authority to open and close the door, but the truth is, Father opens doors that no man can shut and shuts doors that no man can open. Don't be intimidated by the demonic gatekeepers. Don't be fooled. The enemy will not prevail against Father's plans for you!

Exercise the authority Jesus has given you. Demand that the gatekeeper let go in the name of Jesus, and walk with confidence through the doors God opens for you.

MATTHEW 23:13; REVELATION 3:7; JOB 42:2

✦ PRAYER ✦

Thank You for opening the doors that need to be opened for me to walk in Your will. Help me to recognize the doors You are opening and the doors You are closing. Don't let the enemy fool me into walking past a door he's trying to keep shut.

Ask, and It Will Be Given to You

WHAT WOULD HAPPEN if you simply asked? Is it possible that a miracle would manifest in your midst if you only asked? What would happen if you pursued in faith what you think Father is calling you to do? Is it possible you would exceed your own wildest dreams? I'm telling you it *is* possible. Meditate on this: "Ask, and it will be given to you; seek, and you will find; knock, and it will be opened to you. For everyone who asks receives, and he who seeks finds, and to him who knocks it will be opened." You'll never know if you don't ask.

MARK 11:24; MATTHEW 7:7; JAMES 4:3

→ PRAYER ←

Give me a steadfast heart that's persistent in asking, like that of the persistent widow in Luke 18. I refuse to grow weary or faint in releasing my petitions because I believe You are a God who makes the impossible possible, and I know You hear my cries.

LISTEN TO MY VOICE ALONE

*T*HERE ARE MANY voices in the world. Some will encourage you. Some will tear you down. Others will tear you down under the guise of encouraging you. Learn to tune your ear to My voice and My voice alone, even in the words others speak to you.

I promise that I will always lead you down the right path. My path is peaceful. In order to let My peace be the final decision maker in your life, you sometimes have to stop listening to every other voice that would distract you from what I am saying to your heart.

1 CORINTHIANS 14:10; JOHN 10:27; COLOSSIANS 3:15

→ PRAYER ←

Help me to tune out the voices that are not in agreement with Your will. Give me an ear to hear what You are really saying. Help me to discern the wisdom that comes from above and reject the earthly, demonic wisdom that tries to steer me wrong.

Don't Dwell on Negative Thoughts of the Past

Today can be better than yesterday, if you let it. Many times I see you dwelling on the negative thoughts the enemy puts in your mind about yesterday—or last week. My friend, dwelling on thoughts of the past—whether the distant or the recent past—robs you of your ability to enjoy today. The battle is in your mind, and you can win the battle by deliberately choosing to leave the past behind and pressing on toward Father's good plan for today. The enemy may not flee immediately, and he may continue to remind you of your bad yesterday, but you have forever with Jesus—so think on that instead!

HAGGAI 2:9; JOB 8:7; PHILIPPIANS 3:13–14

→ PRAYER ←

Help me to keep eternity in mind—to set my mind on things above and not on the things of this earth—even as I walk through hard days. I commit to leaving yesterday behind and ask You to give me the strength not to dwell on the past.

April

I have yet many things to tell you, but you cannot
bear them now. But when the Spirit of truth comes,
He will guide you into all truth. For He will not
speak on His own authority. But He will speak
whatever He hears, and He will tell you things
that are to come. He will glorify Me, for He will
receive from Me and will declare it to you. All that
the Father has is Mine. Therefore I said that He
will take what is Mine and will declare it to you.

—John 16:12–15

WILL YOU ALLOW ME TO STRETCH YOU?

WILL YOU FULLY yield to Me? Will you submit to My will even when it looks contrary to Your will? Will you allow Me to stretch you in this season? I want to enlarge your capacity to hold spiritual things, but that means letting go of carnal things to make more room for Me. It means cultivating a new harvest of My fruit in your heart.

I want to let My gifts flow through you, but that means you must release the things that hinder My love. Will you allow Me to stretch you? Will you decrease so Jesus can increase in your heart?

JAMES 4:7; ROMANS 8:7; JOHN 3:30

✦ PRAYER ✦

I say yes to You, Holy Spirit. I say yes to Your will and Your ways even when I don't understand Your work in my life. I ask You to enlarge my spiritual capacity, to enlarge my heart to love You more, and to help me surrender all that is getting in the way.

April 2

Follow My Spiritual Warfare Strategy

When it comes to spiritual warfare, there's a time to shout and a time to stay silent. I am the One who gives you the spiritual warfare strategy. I am the One who gives you the blueprint that leads to victory. When you walk in My wisdom in spiritual warfare, you can be sure the enemy will be delivered into your hands.

Sometimes you have to hold your peace, like the Israelites stuck between the Red Sea and the Egyptian army. Other times you have to shout like Joshua at Jericho. Before rushing into battle against your spiritual enemies, ask Me for the strategy. I will lead you to victory.

Exodus 14:13–14; Joshua 6:2–5;
2 Corinthians 2:14

⤞ Prayer ⤝

Show me when it's time to shout and when it's time to stay silent. Show me Your blueprint and Your battle plan and Your timing. I can't fight in my own strength, but Your power and authority always put me in a position to enforce Christ's victory.

April 3

KEEP GETTING BACK UP

I DON'T EXPECT YOU to be perfect. When you fall down, get back up again. Even if you've made the same mistake one thousand times, if you continue to declare war on your wrong behavior, you will eventually gain victory over bad habits. One way to define spiritual warfare is simply "outlasting the devil." So when you sin, repent. If you sin again, repent again. Just keep getting back up. A righteous man falls down seven times and gets back up again.

Don't stop warring against the sin that's warring against you. I will give you the strength to stand against anything and everything that is standing against you—even your flesh. Lean into Me when you feel weak.

PROVERBS 24:16; 1 JOHN 1:9; ACTS 3:19

→ PRAYER ←

When I am weak, You are strong. Help me to lean on Your strength and Your power to do the right thing in the face of every temptation. Thank You for always strengthening me to overcome bad habits and sinful actions by Your grace.

April 4

SEEK TO PLEASE GOD, NOT MAN

*Y*OU CAN'T MAKE everyone happy. One group will be angry if you say one thing, and a second group will be angry if you say another thing. A third group will be angry if you *don't* say something. So stop trying to make everyone happy and focus on pleasing Father. It's really that simple.

People may attack you and gnash their teeth at you as the religious Pharisees gnashed their teeth at the disciple Stephen, but if you are confident you are pleasing Father, then the spiritual warfare, attacks, criticism—and even the praises of man— will roll off your back, and you will have peace and joy in Me. Seek to please Father, not man!

PROVERBS 29:25; GALATIANS 1:10; PROVERBS 16:7

→ PRAYER ←

If I have to choose between pleasing God and pleasing man, I choose pleasing God. Help me always to make that decision, even in the face of angry people who don't understand. Give me the peace that passes understanding as I stand in Your will no matter what.

DON'T WORRY ABOUT ANYTHING

*W*HAT GOOD DOES it do to worry? Think about it for a minute. Jesus said it best in the Sermon on the Mount: He said not to worry about your life—what you will eat or drink or wear. In other words, don't worry about your provision. Don't worry about anything! We've got it all covered.

Yes, there are troubles in life, but it does no good to worry. Worry demonstrates a lack of faith and hinders those things Father is ready and willing to provide. Cast your cares on Jesus because He cares for you. Don't allow yourself to be anxious or stressed by anything the enemy throws your way.

MATTHEW 6:25–34; 1 PETER 5:7;
PHILIPPIANS 4:6–7

→ PRAYER ←

You're right. It does no good to worry, and I know that You care for me watchfully, so I choose to cast my cares on You. Help me not to take those worries and cares back into my heart but to leave them in Your capable hands. I trust You.

April 6

THERE IS NO DEFEAT IN CHRIST

*W*HEN ALL HELL is breaking loose against you, remember that all of heaven is behind you. A host of angels is ministering on your behalf. If you could only see in the spirit realm, like Elisha's servant, you would understand that there are more fighting with you than there are fighting against you. Look at *Me*, not at the enemy. Meditate on the Word rather than listening to the enemy's fearful thoughts.

Celebrate your victory. Don't consider the possibility of defeat. There is no defeat in Christ, and you are in Christ. Run to the battle line with the name of Jesus, and be assured that the devils will bow. Your part is to pray and exercise your authority as I lead you step by step.

HEBREWS 1:14; 2 KINGS 6:8–17; ROMANS 8:37

✦ PRAYER ✦

Thank You that I have Your backup. Thank You for the name of Jesus. Thank You for the weapons of my warfare. Thank You that I can never lose in Christ. Help me to follow Your leading in the midst of every spiritual battle.

EXPECT YOUR FUTURE TO BE
GREATER THAN YOUR PAST

*D*ETERMINE THAT YOUR future will be greater than your past. Determine that you will enter a new season of intimacy with God. Determine that you will let go of those things that lie behind and press toward the mark for the prize of the high calling of God in Christ Jesus.

Stir yourself up in your most holy faith, praying in the Spirit. Expect new. Expect dreams realized. Expect restoration. Expect Me to move in your life. Your determination and expectation and faith will help you realize My best for you today and every day.

HAGGAI 2:9; JUDE 20; PHILIPPIANS 3:12–14

→ PRAYER ←

I want a more intimate relationship with You. Help me to let go of anything that is preventing me from drawing closer to You. Show me what I need to do to prepare myself for what Father wants to do in my life. I am willing and want to be obedient.

KEEP PRESSING IN FOR CHANGE

CHANGE IS A process—and often it's an ugly process. As I am changing you from glory to glory, it's likely that things will look worse before they look better. Don't stop the process when things look ugly. Don't run away from what I am doing in your heart. Keep partnering with Me to work out the change you want to see in your life.

If you keep pressing in for the change I'm leading you into, you will come out on the other side with new gratitude, new perspective, new effectiveness, new blessings, and much more. And remember, you'll never stop changing as long as you are in your physical body. Embrace My work in your life. It is not always fun, but it's worth it.

2 CORINTHIANS 3:18; JOB 22:21; ROMANS 12:1–2

→ PRAYER ←

Right now I present my body as a living sacrifice to You. Change me as You see fit. Renew my mind. Show me my sinful ways that I may turn from them and embrace the transformation. I will not resist Your work.

Start Thinking the Way I Think

*T*HE WEAPONS of spiritual warfare you have are mighty to pull down strongholds. Consider this: Jesus is your rock, your fortress, and your Savior. There is protection in Him. He is your shield, your safe place. The name of the Lord is a strong tower higher than any stronghold the enemy can erect in your mind.

When you stay aligned with My way of thinking, I will guard your mind from the demonic imaginations that work to build a stronghold in your soul. Cast down those imaginations and every thought that tries to exalt itself above My thoughts. Reflect on the Word of God, and you will be less vulnerable to the words of Satan.

2 Corinthians 10:4–5; Psalm 18:2;
Proverbs 18:10

→ PRAYER ←

The Word of God says to cast down imaginations. Help me to discern the vain imaginations that try to erect a stronghold in my mind and fortify wrong belief systems. Teach me to align my thoughts with Yours.

April 10

WIELD THE SWORD OF THE SPIRIT AGAINST THE ENEMY

THINGS OFTEN AREN'T as bad as they appear. The enemy is a master at setting smoke screens and magnifying your circumstances over the Word of God. But My Word never fails. My love never fails. So pick up the sword of the Spirit, wield it with your mouth, and war against the opposition to My Word that is manifesting in your life. That's the good fight of faith. You're fighting to believe. So fight with the Word of God, which renews your mind with the truth and guards your soul against the enemy's lies.

MATTHEW 24:35; EPHESIANS 6:17;
1 TIMOTHY 6:12

→ PRAYER ←

You've never failed me. Your love never fails. Your Word never fails. Help me to see the truth amid the enemy's lies. Help me to stand on that truth when everything around me seems to be shaking. I commit to fighting the good fight of faith with the sword of the Spirit.

BE QUICK TO FORGIVE

*W*HEN YOU ARE angry and frustrated, you have to ask yourself an honest question: Have you let resentment build up in your heart? Unless you are intentional about forgiving—and are quick to forgive—a residue of resentment will build up over your heart the way dirt builds up on a windshield. Over time it will sink down into your heart and form a root of bitterness. Anger and frustration are often rooted in a failure to forgive the little annoyances as they occur. Eventually, the resentment pot boils over. Be quick to forgive— every time you get slightly annoyed. Be quick to forgive.

HEBREWS 12:15; COLOSSIANS 3:13;
1 CORINTHIANS 13:4–7

→ PRAYER ←

Show me any resentment, bitterness, or unfor-
giveness in my heart. I don't want any part
of it. I choose to forgive, and I renounce
wrong thoughts and emotions that are
standing against Your command to forgive.

April 12

GOD KNOWS WHAT YOU CAN HANDLE

THE STATE OF being overwhelmed is not from Me. Father will not put more on you than you can handle. He will not allow more to come on you than you can bear. That's not how We operate. We know your capacity. We know what you can handle. We know what you are ready for.

If you are overwhelmed, you're receiving pressure that is not from Us. You are receiving pressure from man or the enemy of your soul. Reject the pressure of man. Rise up and shake off the enemy's threats. You are a victorious overcomer. Overcome the sense of being overwhelmed now by meditating on Jesus. Trust Him to deal with those pressuring you to do something Father is not calling you to.

1 CORINTHIANS 10:13; JAMES 1:13; PSALM 118:5–6

✦ PRAYER ✦

Thank You for giving me the wisdom to set healthy boundaries in my life. Thank You for giving me the strength to resist the temptation to be overwhelmed and stressed. And thank You for giving me the solution. I will trust in You to help me.

FOCUS ON WHO YOU ARE IN CHRIST

*Y*OU ARE A new creation in Christ. You are defined by what Christ did on the cross— you are saved, healed, delivered, and prosperous in Him. The enemy will put up smoke and mirrors to distract you from this reality. He doesn't want you to know who you really are. He doesn't want you to know who Jesus really is. He wants you to focus on his evil instead of Father's good.

Stay focused on Jesus, who you are in Him, and who He is in you, and you won't fall for the enemy's devices. The revelation of Jesus and who you are in Him is something that will grow deeper and deeper and deeper the more you meditate on Him.

2 CORINTHIANS 5:17; ISAIAH 54:14; 1 JOHN 4:4

→ PRAYER ←

Reveal Jesus to me in a new way. Show me who I am in Christ. Guide me into truth as I meditate on Scripture verses that tell me who I really am and what I can do as a child of God. I want a deeper revelation of who Jesus is and who I am in Him.

WAIT ON ME

Wait on Me. Just wait. Don't move until I tell you to move. Don't act until I show you what to do. Don't speak until you have perfect peace in your heart. Wait on Me. Just wait. My timing is perfect, and I will lead you where you need to go at just the right time so you will find the blessing that awaits you.

I promise you that if you wait on Me, when you do move, act, or speak, you'll do it with My strength and grace. Even your enemies will recognize the anointing on your life. Wait on Me.

PROVERBS 3:5–6; PSALM 33:20–22; LUKE 12:12

✦ PRAYER ✦

Thank You for leading me with Your peace. I won't move until that peace floods my heart. Show me which way to turn, teach me what to say and when, and prepare a table for me in the presence of my enemies. Let Christ be glorified in my life!

LET THE WORD AND THE
SPIRIT GROUND YOU

THE FACT THAT circumstances in your life are spinning round and round doesn't mean you have to spin along with them. When you feel as if you are spinning in circles—like when you are on one of those rides at the fair that make you so dizzy you can't walk straight even after the spinning stops—grab hold of your mind and behold the Word of God. It will ground you in wisdom, peace, joy, and love if you let it.

If you are in the midst of turbulent trials and tribulations, pray in the Spirit and trust that I am releasing the perfect prayer to Father on your behalf. The Word and the Spirit agree. So get in agreement with Us. A threefold cord is not easily broken.

ECCLESIASTES 4:12; 1 JOHN 5:6–7; JOHN 17:17

✦ PRAYER ✦

I get in agreement right now with Your Spirit and Your Word—which are truth. I refuse to elevate my circumstances above Your truth. Help me to walk in Your truth even in the midst of trials and tribulations that work to distract my heart.

RUN TO FATHER WHEN YOU FALL

WHEN YOU STUMBLE, run to Father. Crawl back if you have to. The enemy wants you to run away from Me when you do or say something that grieves Me. Running away will only make it more difficult to rise up in My power and battle against the wrong thoughts, words, and deeds.

Run to Father when you stumble. He is able to make you stand, even if you come to Him with sin on your hands. Your restoration is as quick as your true repentance. There is therefore now no condemnation to those who are in Christ Jesus. Turn to your Redeemer and let Him wash you with the water of His Word once again. He wants to do it.

JUDE 24; 1 JOHN 1:9; ROMANS 8:1

→ PRAYER ←

Thank You for Your willingness to forgive me over and over and over again. Help me to always run to You when I sin in thought, word, or deed so that I can receive Your forgiveness and realign my heart with Yours.

Give Life to God's Thoughts

THE ENEMY DOESN'T have to feed you a constant stream of imaginations. All he has to do is plant the seed. Father created you with an intellect and the ability to reason, but too often your reasoning is watering the wrong seeds. Too often your reasoning is giving life to the enemy's thoughts rather than giving life to My thoughts in your mind.

Gird up the loins of your mind. Stop meditating on the negative words the enemy is speaking to you. Cast down those imaginations and think on things that are pure, lovely, and so on. It will change your mind and better your life.

1 Peter 1:13; 2 Corinthians 10:5;
Philippians 4:8

⋆ Prayer ⋆

I know sometimes my reasoning leads me into confusion, and You are not the author of confusion. Help me guard my mind from the negative thoughts the enemy whispers to my soul and think about Your good plan for my life.

April 18

WAIT FOR MY DIRECTION

ON'T DO ANYTHING until I show you what to do. I know sometimes you feel as if you are in crisis mode, but that's part of the enemy's plan to bring chaos and confusion to your soul. Know and believe this: your heavenly Father is in control. He is not surprised by the things that surprise you. Take a deep breath and get clarity regarding His plan. The devil wants you to run out ahead of Us and make a bigger mess and more mistakes. Resist that temptation. Be still and know that I am God, and wait for My direction. I know the way through, and it's perfect.

PSALM 27:13–14; LAMENTATIONS 3:25;
PSALM 40:1–17

✦ PRAYER ✦

I commit to waiting on You. I will not take a step or move an inch in difficult situations until You reveal the next step. Thank You for always ordering my steps and sharing wisdom from Your heart. Thank You for leading me and guiding me in truth.

LET GO OF FRUSTRATION

ETTING FRUSTRATED TAKES you nowhere fast—except into anxiety, anger, and all manner of ungodly reactions. When you sense that you are getting frustrated, you have stopped receiving My grace. Don't move ahead of Me, and don't question My ability. Take a deep breath and know that I'm going to work it out, whether it's a difficult assignment, an annoying person, or some pain in your body. Let go of the frustration and receive My grace to empower you to move toward your goal. I believe in you, and what frustrates you doesn't frustrate Me. Let My peace overcome you now.

ISAIAH 41:10; JOHN 16:33; ROMANS 8:28

→ PRAYER ←

Holy Spirit, I need Your grace. You are the Spirit of grace. Help me reject the emotion of frustration that causes me to move in the flesh and prevents me from hearing You clearly and receiving Your help. Teach me to walk in Your peace.

April 20

I WANT YOU TO ABIDE IN MY PERFECT LOVE

WHEN YOU BLESS My name, it blesses My heart. When you bless My heart, I bless your heart. We are in complete unity in that moment, blessing one another with a perfect love. That perfect love casts out all fear, casts down all imaginations, and pushes away all cares and worries. That perfect love is the place where I want you to abide, even beyond your times of worship. Your obedience out of a heart of love blesses Me and causes Me to bless you. I want you to walk in the revelation that your blessing Me returns blessing to you and to experience the fruit of My love working in your life.

PSALM 113:2; 1 JOHN 4:18; JOHN 14:23

✦ PRAYER ✦

I want to abide in Your perfect love—such a glorious place to dwell! I bless You with all that is within me. I bless Your name and pledge my allegiance to You. Will You help me walk every moment in the perfect love Scripture describes?

Don't Hold Grudges Against the Judases in Your Life

We all run into Judases in our lives. But remember, Jesus did not hold a grudge against Judas. He knew the Father was going to use his betrayal for the greater good. Jesus did not lash out against Judas. He submitted everything to Father's will, and in the end the betrayal led to the salvation of many.

Everyone runs into Judases. Will you hold a grudge, resist Father's work through the pain, and lash out? Or will you submit it all to God and believe He works all things together for good to those who love Him and are called according to His purposes? Lives may depend on your response.

Luke 22:48; Luke 22:42; Romans 8:28

→ Prayer ←

I submit my heart and my life to Your will. When I am betrayed or maligned, help me to respond according to Your ways and not the ways of my flesh. Help me to be quick to forgive even those—and especially those—who are closest to me.

April 22

HAVE AN ETERNAL VIEW OF YOUR LIFE

*S*UDDENLIES: SOME ARE good, and others are devastating. No matter what type you are experiencing, remain fixed on Jesus. Avoid the emotional roller coaster that circumstances build. Whether you suddenly received the best news of your life or the worst, remember that this world fades away. Only faith, hope, and love abide.

Take Christ's perspective. Have an eternal view of your life. Remain fixed on My purposes. Circumstances come and go, but the Word of God endures forever. Circumstances will change for better or worse, but Jesus never changes. Stay fixed on Him. You have the victory in *every* suddenly!

1 CORINTHIANS 13:13; MALACHI 3:6;
HEBREWS 13:8

✦ PRAYER ✦

Your hope is the anchor of my soul. Your Word stabilizes my emotions in the good times and the bad. Help me to maintain a steadfast gaze on You and to keep an eternal perspective when I face the "suddenlies" that are sure to come into my life.

CHOOSE TO LET PEACE RULE IN YOUR HEART

ESUS PUT IT plainly when He said to let the peace of God rule in your heart. You have Jesus's peace—perfect, undisturbed peace—in your heart because Jesus left you His peace.

When disturbances come, you have a choice. You have to choose to "let" Jesus's peace rule in your heart. In other words, Jesus has done His part: He gave you His peace. Now you have to do your part: you have to allow that peace to rule. Reject every assignment from the enemy to rob your peace. Commit to a lifestyle of peace. You'll be more powerful as a result.

COLOSSIANS 3:15; JOHN 14:27;
2 THESSALONIANS 3:16

✦ PRAYER ✦

The world is not peaceful, but You are. I crave Your peace. Give me a deeper revelation of the peace Jesus left me, and help me to resist the temptation to abandon peace and walk in the chaos of this age. You are my peace.

April 24

QUICKLY DISCERN THE ENEMY'S DEVICES

WHEN YOU KEEP running into the same roadblock over and over, something is wrong somewhere. I can help you. Usually it's a wrong thought pattern, but sometimes it's the enemy using the same old tricks to stop you. When you are willing to allow something to stop you, whether it's a bad headache or an argument at home, the enemy will continue using that same tactic to stop you next time around. That's why you need to discern the demonic pattern and press through the resistance. Only you can let the devil stop you. So renew your mind, and don't be ignorant of the enemy's devices. I am here to help you.

2 CORINTHIANS 2:11; HEBREWS 5:14;
PROVERBS 18:15

✦ PRAYER ✦

You see and know all things. Help me to discern the obstacles in my path, whether they are the enemy's devices or just my flesh warring against You. I want to walk in Your perfect plan. Help me press through any and all resistance to Your will.

Don't Draw Back!

Sometimes I see you drawing back because you are weary from the battle. I understand your withdrawing, but I have something to say about it: rise up because the victory is yours. Refuse to allow the enemy to slow you down, cause you to turn to the right or the left, or put you in a corner. Rise up in the power of My might, and I will show Myself strong on your behalf.

Jesus has put your enemies to shame with the Cross. Embrace the work of the Cross, and you will walk boldly in the face of all who oppose you. The righteous are as bold as a lion. So don't draw back. Rise up. I am with you.

Isaiah 60:1; Ephesians 6:10; Proverbs 28:1

↦ Prayer ↤

Thank You for the power of Your might! I will rise up in Your strength with the assurance that You have given me the victory. Help me to lean on You and not my own strength as I walk through this dark world trying to accomplish Your will.

April 26

BE WILLING TO WRESTLE

*T*OO MANY CHRISTIANS put a premature period after "wrestle" in Ephesians 6:12 (NKJV). They stop after the phrase "we do not wrestle." But you must realize you are in a spiritual war against principalities and powers. You are a citizen in the kingdom of God, and the demons in the kingdom of darkness plot against you. If you do not wrestle—if you do not exercise your authority in Christ—you will not walk in the complete victory Christ won for you. Don't focus excessively on the enemy, but don't take him for granted either. There are spiritual strongholds over your city and maybe even over your life. Run quickly to the battle line when I lead you because your victory is certain.

EPHESIANS 6:12–20; PHILIPPIANS 3:20;
1 SAMUEL 17:48

→ PRAYER ←

My citizenship is in heaven. I am seated in heavenly places in Christ Jesus. Remind me of that when things on this earth seem to contradict the victory I know is mine. Give me the wisdom to go forth in battle to enforce Christ's victory.

KEEP CHIPPING AWAY AT IT

*J*UST KEEP CHIPPING away at whatever's resisting you or blocking your path. Even if you don't see progress with your natural eyes, you are making a dent in the spirit. Think about this: if you take a whack at a tree with an ax ten times a day, that tree will eventually fall. It may take longer than you would like, but sooner or later, the tree will come down.

This principle holds true in the spiritual realm also. If you don't give up, what is resisting you will eventually fall. If you keep pressing into what I have told you to do, even if you don't see visible results, you will break through. Keep chipping away.

GALATIANS 6:9; LUKE 11:9–10;
2 THESSALONIANS 3:13

→ PRAYER ←

Help me resist the temptation to give up when I'm weary. Give me a persistent, persevering spirit in the face of obstacles in the spirit and in the flesh. Help me walk by faith and not by sight so I won't get discouraged by what doesn't look right.

April 28

Believe That God Is at Work

Things may look much different tomorrow, so hold your peace. Don't make any decisions today, and don't be discouraged. Many times when hell is breaking loose against you, the enemy backs off as quickly as he came if you just stay steady. The key is not to get sucked into the drama. You do that by believing wholeheartedly that Father is in control, by casting your cares on Jesus, by asking for My help, and by believing that We are going to work it all together for good and that you will emerge victorious, stronger, and wiser for the experience.

James 1:19; Isaiah 59:19; 1 Peter 5:7;
2 Corinthians 4:17–18

→ Prayer ←

When the enemy comes in like a flood, raise up a standard against him! Help me to remember that this too shall pass. Help me to lock on to Your Word in the midst of the warfare, to be quick to listen to Your voice, and to be slow to speak from my soul.

You Don't Have to Respond

Sometimes no response is the best response. When someone attacks you verbally, sometimes it's wise to remain silent. Sometimes you can explain with a soft answer and hope it turns away the person's wrath. But sometimes no response is the best response.

Don't meditate on the negativity. Turn to Father and pray for the person attacking you. It could be that he will return to you with an apology. Or it could be that he'll attack you more because he doesn't think the first attack got your attention. Either way, you've moved in the opposite spirit, and Father is pleased. Don't respond to the attack unless I give you the words to say. In the meantime stay prayerful.

Matthew 26:63; Mark 14:61; 1 Peter 3:9

→ Prayer ←

Set a guard over my mouth. Keep watch over the doors of my lips. Do not let my heart fret because it leads only to evil. Help me to resist the temptation to repay evil with evil or railing for railing or insult for insult. Help me not to respond.

April 30

WHAT WAITING ON THE LORD REALLY MEANS

*I*F YOU WAIT on the Lord, your strength will be renewed. That is Our promise. But We won't do your part. You have to do the waiting.

What does it mean to wait on the Lord? It means sitting in My presence. It means gazing on Jesus's beauty. It means not rushing ahead of Me to try to fix the crisis that's draining your strength. It means waiting in expectation for Me to show up and conquer your enemies for you, vindicate you, or promote you. When you lean completely on Me and not on your own understanding, you are in a strong position. Indeed, My strength is made perfect in your weakness.

ISAIAH 40:31; PSALM 27:4; PROVERBS 3:5–6

→ PRAYER ←

I don't want to rush ahead of You. Engage my heart with Your love so that I will not move without Your leading. Give me such sensitivity to Your Spirit that I will be unwilling to move unless You do. Thank You for teaching me what it means to wait on the Lord.

May

When the day of Pentecost had come, they were all together in one place. Suddenly a sound like a mighty rushing wind came from heaven, and it filled the whole house where they were sitting. There appeared to them tongues as of fire, being distributed and resting on each of them, and they were all filled with the Holy Spirit and began to speak in other tongues, as the Spirit enabled them to speak.

—ACTS 2:1–4

MY POWER DWELLS IN YOU

SOMETIMES YOU NEED to take a step back and breathe. That's OK. Breathe. Father gives you the breath of life. I live in you and empower you. Don't take Our life and Our power for granted. Meditate on them and you will feel My strength rising up in your heart.

Consider this: the Spirit that raised Christ from the dead dwells in you. Your fervent, effective prayers make tremendous power available to you. You don't yet realize how powerful you truly are in Christ. I'm telling you that no devil can stop you. Take a deep breath, and then get up and pursue Father's will for your life. I am with you.

JOB 33:4; ROMANS 8:11; JAMES 5:16

→ PRAYER ←

*I refuse to take Your empowerment for granted,
but I will meditate on Your indwelling in
my spirit until I know that I know that I
know that You are with me. Show me the
mighty power I have as a child of God so
that my confidence in God will rise.*

May 2

KEEP PRESSING INTO THE KINGDOM

THE KINGDOM OF heaven suffers violence, and the violent take it by force. This truth implies that a spiritual war is raging, with resisting forces that stand between you and Father's will for your life, for your family, and for the earth. Do you want to be an overcomer? Press into the kingdom, and when you've pressed in all you can, press in a little harder.

I will empower you to keep pressing toward Father's perfect will for your life. If you don't quit, you'll win. You can't lose if you keep pressing into the kingdom. You have victory in Christ. See it and you will live it.

MATTHEW 11:12; JAMES 4:7; PHILIPPIANS 2:13

✣ PRAYER ✣

I will submit myself to Father and resist the devil and all his schemes by Your power. Help me to press past the resistance in the spirit realm. Help me to press past my flesh that wars against You. Help me to keep on pressing in no matter what.

YOU ARE "MORE THAN" IN CHRIST

ON'T LET ANYONE make you feel "less than." Family. Friends. Christian brothers and sisters. Sometimes they put you down to lift themselves up. Sometimes they know what they are doing, and sometimes they don't. Regardless, the truth is that no one can "make" you feel "less than" when you know who you are in Christ. When your identity is rooted and grounded in Christ, words that try to make you feel "less than" won't matter because you are confident that you are "more than" a conqueror in Him. As for those who put you down, move in the opposite spirit and lift them up. Bless them, and you will be blessed.

COLOSSIANS 2:7; ROMANS 8:37; ROMANS 12:14

✦ PRAYER ✦

I refuse to compare myself to others or receive the negative words people say about me. My identity is firmly rooted in Christ. Help me to see myself and others the way You see me so that I will edify myself and others with my words.

May 4

ALL GOD'S PROMISES ARE YES AND AMEN

RENEW THE COMMITMENT in your heart to be a doer of the Word, and you will receive tremendous blessings, including peace and joy in the midst of your trials. As you mature in Christ, becoming more and more like Him, you will see with your own eyes just how true Father's promises really are. All of His promises are yes and amen. Seeing that truth manifest in your life is largely a matter of persevering despite what your circumstances tempt you to believe. The alternative to walking in faith is being double-minded, and a double-minded man is unstable in all his ways.

JAMES 1:22; 2 CORINTHIANS 1:20; JAMES 1:8

✦ PRAYER ✦

I believe Your promises and refuse to be moved off the truth in Your Word. Help me to stay the course no matter what I might see with my natural eyes. Help me to keep my mind stayed on Christ and walk in His peace as I wait for Father's promises.

Hand Me the Reins

I want to help you. I am your helper. But sometimes you won't take your hands off what you're dealing with. I can't get involved at the level I want to until you take your hands off and give the situation to Jesus. As long as you are striving in the flesh to fix something, get something, or get rid of something, you are not allowing My grace to work in your life the way I intend it to.

I am going to show you some areas of your life in which I want you to hand Me the reins. If you'll give them to Me, I will take the lead and show you the steps to take to work things out. I am waiting for you to get to the end of yourself so I can show Myself strong in your life.

John 14:26; Psalm 38:15; 2 Chronicles 16:9

✦ Prayer ✦

Show me now where You want me to take my hands off the reins, and I will do it. Help me to see where I am getting in Your way, and I will get out of Your way. Teach me Your ways and show me Your paths. I commit my heart to yielding to You.

LEARN THE DIFFERENCE BETWEEN CONVICTION AND CONDEMNATION

*W*HEN THE ENEMY is attacking, it's important to check your heart and ensure that you didn't open the door to him. But know this: the enemy will try to make you feel as if you've done something wrong even when you haven't. I *convict*; the enemy *condemns*. I want to teach you how to distinguish between conviction of sin and condemnation. One way to discern the difference is that conviction comes from My heart of love for you. I am love, and I will not condemn you for a sin that opens the door to the enemy. Just repent.

ROMANS 8:1; ROMANS 8:34; JOHN 8:10–11

→ PRAYER ←

I welcome Your conviction, Holy Spirit, because I want to walk circumspectly before You. Help me to discern Your heart of love and avoid the snare of condemnation the enemy lays out for me when I fall short of Your glory.

The Truth Will Set You Free

*W*HERE THE SPIRIT of God is, there is liberty! Pursue a greater awareness of My presence in your midst, and you will break free from the oppressive thoughts that hold you back from My perfect will for your life. I am with you. I live in you. I will never leave you or forsake you!

The more you reflect on these truths, the more powerful you will be. Ask Me for a greater revelation of them as you meditate on Father's Word. As you apply your heart to understand, I will pour out the wisdom and revelation you desire, and the truth will set you free.

2 CORINTHIANS 3:17; 1 CORINTHIANS 6:19;
PROVERBS 2:2

→ PRAYER ←

Give me a greater revelation of Your presence and clear discernment of the enemy's work to plant oppressive thoughts in my soul. Give me understanding that You live in me and will never leave me. Show me the truth that will set me free!

May 8

Be Prepared for the Enemy

*T*aking a defensive stance doesn't mean expecting the worst. It simply means being prepared for anything and everything the enemy may send your way. If you're expecting the blow, it won't impact you nearly as much as if you are blindsided.

Be prepared by staying in fellowship Me, renewing your mind with the Word, and pursuing Father's heart. Expect the best every day, but stay alert because your enemy is roaming about like a roaring lion seeking someone to devour. It doesn't have to be you! I'll warn you if you stay near to My heart.

1 Corinthians 16:13; 1 Peter 5:8; 1 Peter 1:13

→ Prayer ←

Give me an alert spirit so that I will be quick to hear Your warnings. Help me to stay vigilant and watchful, not because I fear the enemy but because Your Word commands it. I commit my heart to stay in close fellowship with You all my days.

Pray for Those Who Persecute You

Wʜᴇɴ ꜱᴏᴍᴇᴏɴᴇ ꜱᴘᴇᴀᴋꜱ unkind words about you or your family, the devil will do everything he can to make sure they get back to your ears. Talking down about people is called gossip, and I hate it. You have two choices when you hear the unkind words: you can react in the same wicked spirit, or you can resist the temptation and act like your Father in heaven.

I say to you, let no corrupt talk come out of your mouth. Build people up even if they tear you down. Pray for those who persecute you and say all manner of evil against you so you can be like Jesus.

Pʀᴏᴠᴇʀʙꜱ 16:28; Jᴀᴍᴇꜱ 3:5; Eᴘʜᴇꜱɪᴀɴꜱ 4:29;
Mᴀᴛᴛʜᴇᴡ 5:44

✦ Prayer ✦

I don't like to hear gossip and slander about me or anyone else. Help me not to engage in it. Help me to speak the truth in love no matter what unlovely things are said about me. For Christ's sake, give me a heart to pray for those who gossip about me.

May 10

ACT LIKE WHO YOU REALLY ARE

*D*O YOU REALLY know who you are in Christ? You are more than a conqueror, even in times of trial. You are accepted in the beloved, even though you make mistakes. You are holy and blameless before Him, even while you're growing. Rise up in your identity and act like who you really are, and you'll find more peace, joy, and victory in your life. Take on a righteousness-consciousness rather than a sin-consciousness. Look at who you are in Christ instead of what the enemy wants to show you about yourself. It's vital that you understand who you really are and how much We love you.

ROMANS 8:37; EPHESIANS 1:4–6; ROMANS 5:17

→ PRAYER ←

I am often hard on myself. Help me to focus on who I am in Christ rather than on what I don't do right. Help me to be quick to repent when I fall short of Your glory and to realize that You love me despite my shortcomings. Show me who I really am.

Mornings With the Holy Spirit

WAIT UNTIL THE TRIAL IS OVER TO MAKE DECISIONS

*D*on't make major decisions in the midst of a trial. With so much natural and spiritual pressure, it can be difficult to make the right ones. The enemy comes in with destructive emotions that toss you to and fro in your soul. By meditating on the Word of God, you will anchor your soul with hope that breeds faith. You will find stability in the middle of the torrent. Unless you have a clear word from Me, put off major decisions until the trial is over. I promise you: things will look much different when you have My perspective.

Hebrews 6:19; Romans 10:17; Proverbs 3:5–6

→ PRAYER ←

Give me wisdom to make right decisions according to the Word of God and Your understanding. Stabilize the emotions that run deep in the midst of fiery trials so that I can hear Your voice clearly and obey Your instructions.

WHEN A STORM IS RAGING, FOCUS ON JESUS

WHEN A STORM is raging against you, you have two choices: focus on the wind or focus on Jesus. If you choose to focus on the wind, you will be tossed to and fro by the fears in your soul. If you choose to focus on Jesus, to meditate on His Word, and to speak it out of your mouth, you will find peace even if the winds don't immediately die down. And the winds will die down in time. Don't focus on the wind.

MATTHEW 7:25; MARK 4:35–41; ISAIAH 26:3

✦ PRAYER ✦

Help me to keep Jesus at the center of my focus no matter what is going on around me. Teach me how to draw from His peace and allow Him to calm the storm in my soul that rises up when the winds of trials and tribulations blow in my life.

IT'S OK TO REST

*N*EVER GIVE UP! I won't let you. But it's OK to rest in Jesus. Yes, sometimes it's OK to let your foot off the gas and just cruise in My grace. Don't press so hard toward your goals that you burn out. Move at the pace I've set for you, and you will feel the anointing and recognize the grace to move. I want to teach you how to flow in My grace and tap into the wisdom of rest. Resting and reassessing your situation is not giving up. You will find new strength and new strategies to be more effective in Christ if you slow down when I tell you to.

MARK 6:31; PSALM 127:2; HEBREWS 4:9–11

✦ PRAYER ✦

I choose to rest in Jesus and resist the temptation to keep pressing past the grace that You've given me. Teach me how to recognize both Your anointing to press on and Your guidance to stop and rest awhile. Give me wisdom to know when to reassess.

May 14

SEEK TO PLEASE GOD ALONE

ANY PEOPLE WILL judge you wrongly. As soon as Father promotes you, you'll meet folks who will tell you something they believe you are doing wrong and judge your heart. You can't please man, so don't try. Give heed to and pray about the advice that comes from those with whom you are in relationship. They know you best. Don't let attacks from strangers stop you.

Ultimately I am the one to convict you of sin, so stay close to Me, and I will show you if you are moving in the wrong direction. Seek to please Father and Him alone. He will take care of the rest.

MATTHEW 10:28; 1 CORINTHIANS 4:3;
1 CORINTHIANS 2:15

→ PRAYER ←

I refuse to bow to the fear of man. I will fear the Lord and Him only. Surround me with wise counselors who hear Your voice, and guard me from the temptation to be a people pleaser. Help me to guard my heart diligently and to be quick to repent.

Keep Your Eyes on Me

Stop looking at your shortcomings and look at Me. When you keep your eyes on Me, you tap into My grace and power to overcome the ways of your flesh that leave you feeling guilty and condemned. Guilt and condemnation do not come from Me; they come from the enemy.

Arise, burn, and shine! Don't let the enemy keep you down, cover you with his darkness, or put out your fire. Father wants to use you in a new way! Repent, shake off the guilt, and arise in the name of Jesus. My grace and strength are available to you.

John 16:8; Romans 7:15–19; Micah 7:19

✦ Prayer ✦

I will not heed the voice of the accuser of the brethren. Help me not to give in to feelings of guilt and shame after I grieve You with my words and deeds. Thank You for casting my sin into the depths of the sea and for strengthening my heart.

Follow My Leading in Ministering to Others

*T*HERE'S A FINE line between showing compassion and rescuing people from consequences they need to face in order to learn and grow. Moving in soulish compassion is not My will for you—or for those you are trying help. Moving in Jesus's compassion is the best way to help people. Moving in works of the soul or works of the flesh can hinder the help that I want to deliver. I love your heart to help people, but ask Me first. I will show you the line between soulish compassion and spiritual compassion so you can act according to My will.

PROVERBS 19:19; PROVERBS 1:7; PSALM 18:30

→ PRAYER ←

I know that You love people even more than I do. Help me to stay out of Your way and to avoid trying to solve problems that You have not called me to solve. Help me to show Your compassion in Your way and in Your timing.

REMAIN STABLE AS SEASONS CHANGE

*S*EASONS NEVER LAST. There are turbulent seasons and seasons in which you feel as if you are on top of the world. The keyword is *stability*. Whether a new season brings increase or challenges, rely on Me to help you remain stable and vigilant. The enemy is always roaming about like a roaring lion seeking whom he may devour. But Jesus has already delivered you from the mouth of the lion. So stand strong and rejoice as your season shifts. Victory belongs to you.

ECCLESIASTES 3:1; 2 TIMOTHY 4:17; PSALM 139:16

⇝ PRAYER ⇜

Teach me how to remain constant no matter what the season. Show me how to walk through each season of my life with a wisdom and stability that will speak to those who don't yet know Jesus. Give me a keen spirit to avoid the snares of the enemy.

May 18

WILL YOU YIELD TO ME?

*J*AM YOUR COMFORTER. But I will draw you out of your natural comfort zone to encourage spiritual growth. Don't resist My leading, My words of wisdom, or My stretching. I know it doesn't feel good to your flesh—your flesh wars against My Spirit—but I promise you this: if you commit to decrease in your flesh so that Jesus can increase in your heart, you will realize greater peace, greater comfort, and greater joy in your life. Will you yield to Me even when it hurts?

GALATIANS 5:17; JOHN 3:30; ROMANS 6:13

→ PRAYER ←

I don't like change, but I commit to following You out of my comfort zone because I know the place You are leading me to is good. Help me to remember it's a good place when my flesh defies my mind and my emotions defy my will. I want to yield to You.

Ask Me for the Key

*I*t takes only one key to start your car. It takes only one key to open your house. And it takes only one key to get to a new spiritual level. Here's the good news: I have the key to each level! I see the end from the beginning. I know where Father wants to take you. I know which doors to open and where your breakthroughs will be. I have every key you will ever need to fulfill your destiny. I will give you the right key at the right time. Don't get ahead of Me, and don't lag behind Me. Keep asking Me for the key you need to open the door to the next phase of your journey.

Isaiah 46:9–11; Isaiah 46:10; Revelation 22:13

→ Prayer ←

*Please give me the keys I need to open the doors
Father has ordained for me to walk through.
Show me which way to turn—and which way
not to turn—so that I will experience the breakthroughs You've prepared for me. I set my heart
to follow You at the pace You determine.*

May 20

WAIT UPON THE LORD

*Y*OU'VE HEARD IT said—and indeed I've told you before—to wait upon the Lord. Waiting on the Lord is not merely about being patient. It is not merely about refusing to move ahead without My leading. Waiting on the Lord is an active pursuit of Father's will. Waiting on the Lord is eagerly expecting Me to show up in the midst of your circumstances to tell you exactly what to do and what to say at a particular time. When you wait on Me—no matter how long you have to wait—you will have joy because of your certainty that I am going to show up.

PSALM 27:14; 1 CHRONICLES 16:11;
HEBREWS 11:6; PSALM 25:4–5

✤ PRAYER ✦

Thank You for teaching me how to wait on You. I want to move in Father's perfect will and perfect timing. I set my heart to eagerly wait on the Lord, seek His face, and expect Him to break in with everything I need to do His will.

TO CALM THE STORM

*W*HAT YOU ARE going through isn't going to last forever. Like a hurricane, it will pass, and you will recover your power again. The truth is, you haven't lost your power. You just feel powerless because of the enemy's onslaught. So focus on the power that raised Christ from the dead that dwells in you and get back up again. Focus on Me. I am your intercessor, your Advocate, your standby, your Comforter, and your counselor. I am everything to you that Jesus was to His disciples in the midst of the raging storm He spoke to. I'll give you the words to speak to your storm. Only believe.

JOHN 16:7; 2 TIMOTHY 1:7; 1 CORINTHIANS 4:20

✦ PRAYER ✦

The power that raised Christ from the
dead dwells in me! Therefore I am able to
meet every challenge that comes my way
in Christ. Give me the words to speak to
the storms that rage in my life. I choose to
believe I am who Your Word says I am.

May 22

BE JOYOUS BOTH ON THE PEAKS AND IN THE VALLEYS

REMEMBER WHAT IT was like being on top of the mountain? You felt as if you were on top of the world! In reality you *are* on top of the world, even when it doesn't feel as if you are. The world has no power to hold you down. However, trials will come to perfect your character.

Peaks and valleys are part of your walk with Me—times of triumph as well as times of trial. The promised land is filled with peaks and valleys. Always remember the joy of the mountaintop, and refuse to let go of it when a valley rises up to meet you.

ISAIAH 54:10; PSALM 23:4; LUKE 3:5

⬧ PRAYER ⬧

Even when I walk through the valley of the shadow of death, I will fear no evil. And when I am on the mountaintop, I will continue to seek Your face. Help me to remain content in Christ whether I am in a valley or on a mountaintop.

HELP OTHERS AS I LEAD

*F*ATHER WILL MAKE a way where there seems to be no way. Jesus is the way. I know the way. We have you completely covered. It's not possible for you to fall out of Our grip. We are one with you. So get your mind off the circumstances that defy this reality. Get your mind on helping someone else while We help you.

What you make happen for someone else, We will make happen for you. So look to Me and seek to help others as I lead. Everything else will fall into place. It really will. Die to yourself and live for Us. We've got it all figured out. Just rest in Me.

JOHN 14:6; JOHN 10:29; EPHESIANS 6:8

✦ PRAYER ✦

I don't always see the way, but I trust the One who does. Your way is always good. Show me how to walk in Your way. Help me to instruct others in Your way so they can walk on Your good path. I am depending on Your guidance.

May 24

Put on the Whole Armor of God

THE PERSON WHO desires to walk in true authority must put on the *whole* armor of God to wrestle against principalities and powers. That armor consists of more than a sword. Righteousness, truth, faith, and peace are essential to wielding spiritual authority. Never compromise in those areas because you will compromise your efficacy.

And do not fail to walk in love. Your shield of faith will be stronger because faith works by love. Love should be the motive for everything you do—even engaging in spiritual warfare. Your authority in Christ is rooted in His love for you. He wants you to use it to push back anything that hinders people from experiencing His love.

EPHESIANS 6:12; EPHESIANS 5:2; GALATIANS 5:6

✦ Prayer ✦

Remind me to put on the whole armor of God. Help me to walk in true spiritual authority without compromise. Give me a heart for intercession that leads to intimacy with You and helps others enter into a deeper relationship with Jesus. Let Your love constrain me.

BREAK OLD SOUL TIES

SOMETIMES OLD ASSOCIATIONS need to be severed. I understand why you are reluctant to lay the ax to the root of rotten relationships. You don't want to hurt anyone. I love that about you. But if you don't do it, people will hinder the harvest of blessings in your life.

Obey My voice. I know where Father is taking you—and He has a more abundant life in mind for you. So when I show you it's time to break a soul tie, break it and don't look back. Rest assured that you'll be blessed by your obedience, and I will take care of the one I've told you to leave behind.

GENESIS 19:26; DEUTERONOMY 28; JOHN 10:10

→ PRAYER ←

Show me the ties I need to break and the ties I need to strengthen to see Your blessings over-take me. No matter how much it hurts to let go of old associations that are poisoning my soul, strengthen me to obey Your voice.

I Am Calling You as an Agent of Unity

I AM CALLING YOU as an agent of My unity in this hour. Jesus is building His church, and surely the gates of hell will not prevail against it. But the division among My people and among the churches is causing a breach that prevents Me from moving the way I want to move. Pave the way to unity with humility, grace, and love. Seek to be a peacemaker. Trumpet the message of unity but also walk in it. It won't be easy, but I will empower you to do it. It is vital for you to work for unity in this hour.

PHILIPPIANS 2:2; 1 PETER 3:8; ROMANS 12:4–5

⇢ PRAYER ⇠

Your heart cries out for unity, so I unite my heart with Yours and embrace Your call to repair the breaches in Your church. Show me what to do, where to go, whom to talk to—and how to pray—to see unity manifest among Your people in this hour.

WALK IN THE SPIRIT

No weapon formed against you shall prosper. But that doesn't mean the weapon won't come against you. And it doesn't mean you can't give it the power to distract you. You can allow the enemy a measure of success in your life by having an emotional reaction to the attack rather than wholeheartedly trusting Me. Cancel the devil's ability to prosper in your soul by focusing on My saving grace in the attack he has launched. Walk in the Spirit, and the enemy will not prosper in your soul.

ISAIAH 54:17; PSALM 91; GALATIANS 5:16

→ PRAYER ←

Help me walk in the Spirit all the days of my life. I don't want to fulfill the lusts of the flesh. I don't want to be led forth by emotions. I want to be led forth by You. Show me how to crucify my flesh and rein in my emotions for Your glory.

May 28

Pursue Lasting Change in Your Heart

*L*ASTING CHANGE COMES when you are willing to see yourself as I see you. At times that means seeing, acknowledging, and repenting for a wrong thought that's hindering love. Other times it means confessing a sinful word or deed that's hindering fellowship with Me. But it always means seeing My love for you in spite of it all.

My goodness will lead you to the change we both want to see in your heart—but that change will happen only when you see where you are and how that conflicts with where I want to take you. Embrace My glorious work in your soul. I have the power to help you become more like your beautiful Savior.

1 JOHN 1:9; EPHESIANS 4:24; EPHESIANS 2:10;
JOHN 15:16

✦ PRAYER ✦

I want to see myself the way You see me. I repent of my sins in thought and deed and ask You to forgive me and restore me to perfect fellowship with You. Thank You that You love me with an undying love and that You are changing me little by little.

Think About My Love for You

When you think about Me, remember how pure My love for you is. Consider the fact that every word I speak to your heart is motivated by love. My thoughts toward you are full of love. I lead you and guide you by the law of love. There's nothing you can do or say to cause My great love for you to wane. So come closer to My heart. Listen to My words of love and let them encourage your heart, let them strengthen your soul, let them inspire you to lay your life down for Christ's Great Commission.

1 Corinthians 13:4–8; 1 John 4:10;
Psalm 36:10–12

☩ Prayer ☩

You are love, and everything You do is loving. Thank You for speaking words of love and words of life to my heart. Help me to remember Your words of love when I disappoint myself—and disappoint You—so I will run back into Your arms of love.

May 30

I Want You to Know My Heart

I WANT YOU TO know My heart the way I know your heart. When you truly understand the motives of My heart, when you truly understand how much I care for you, when you get the revelation of My deep love for you, you will never be the same. Our fellowship will be even sweeter and our communion stronger. That's what I want, and I know that's the desire of your heart. I want you to know My heart.

JAMES 1:17; JOHN 3:16; MATTHEW 7:9–11

✦ PRAYER ✦

I want to know Your heart. Reveal Your heart to me directly and through Your Word so that I can comprehend Your great love for me at another level. I want to know by experience how You feel about me. I want to taste and see Your goodness.

DISCERN THE DIFFERENCE
BETWEEN SPIRIT AND FLESH

*N*OT EVERY OBSTACLE you face involves spiritual warfare—but sometimes you don't discern the enemy's coming against you. When you feel as if you can't go another step, it's possible that you are moving beyond My grace. My grace is sufficient to empower you to move in Father's will.

It's also possible that you are being attacked by the enemy, who comes to weary the saints. I want to teach you to discern the source of your discouragement, discontent, and fatigue so you will know whether to pull back and wait on Me or rise up and launch a counterattack in the name of Jesus.

2 CORINTHIANS 12:9; DANIEL 7:25;
2 CORINTHIANS 2:11

→ PRAYER ←

I don't want to be ignorant of the devil's devices, but I don't want to see a devil behind every doorknob, either. Would You help me to stay balanced? Would You help me discern the root of the resistance? I want to move in step with Your plan for my life.

June

There are various gifts, but the same Spirit. There are differences of administrations, but the same Lord. There are various operations, but it is the same God who operates all of them in all people. But the manifestation of the Spirit is given to everyone for the common good. To one is given by the Spirit the word of wisdom, to another the word of knowledge by the same Spirit, to another faith by the same Spirit, to another gifts of healings by the same Spirit, to another the working of miracles, to another prophecy, to another discerning of spirits, to another various kinds of tongues, and to another the interpretation of tongues. But that one and very same Spirit works all these, dividing to each one individually as He will.

—1 Corinthians 12:4–11

You Can Talk to Me Anytime

*Y*ou can talk to Me any time. You know where to find Me. When you engage with My heart, I will engage with yours. You will sense My presence as you draw near to Me. The more you seek Me, the more you will realize that I am right there with you. I am always there, but sometimes the hurried pace of life distracts you from that reality. If you slow down for just a minute and think about Me, joy and peace will arise.

James 4:8; Psalm 119:15; Psalm 139:7

✦ Prayer ✦

Help me to slow down and recognize Your presence no matter how hectic my days are. You are nearer than I know—but I want to know. I want to experience Your presence as I walk through my day. I want to walk with You. Show me how.

June 2

Allow Me to Sanctify You

I AM CALLED "HOLY" for a reason. And you are called to be holy as I am holy. But striving for holiness will not bring you the sanctification you and I desire. You can consecrate yourself unto Father, but I am the One who sanctifies you, regenerates you, and empowers you to walk in My holiness and Christ's righteousness. Stop working so hard, and start speaking and thinking and walking in My Word by My grace. I will do the rest.

LEVITICUS 20:7–8; 1 THESSALONIANS 4:7;
2 TIMOTHY 2:21

→ PRAYER ←

I know You won't do my part, but I can't do Your part, so I am going to stop trying to change myself. Show me my part as I set my heart to enter a new level of Your holiness. Help me to rest in Your holiness and lean into Your transforming power.

Delight in Me as I Delight in You

I DELIGHT IN YOU. Yes, I delight in you. I delight in your prayers, and I delight in your worship. I delight in you most when you delight in Me. For we are one, but when you delight in Me and I delight in You, our communion reaches new heights and our joy in one another is full.

When you delight in Me, I will give you the desires of your heart. And when your desires are for more of Me, I will satisfy your longing and give you more than you could ever hope for.

ZEPHANIAH 3:17; PSALM 147:11; PROVERBS 15:8; PSALM 37:4

✦ Prayer ✦

I delight in You. I delight in praying with You and worshipping You. Show me how to enter the place of delight, not just in times of prayer or worship, but as I walk through everyday life. Help me to continually delight in Your love.

YOU ARE CALLED FOR SUCH A TIME AS THIS

*Y*OU ARE NOT only part of a chosen generation; you are called for such a time as this—for such an hour as this. When I formed you in your mother's womb, I saw your end—I saw your destiny fulfilled. Walk forth with a confidence in your heart that I am with you and guiding you through the valleys and over the hills and from victory to victory into the destiny Father has planned for you. It's a walk of faith that you are gifted to walk.

1 PETER 2:9; ESTHER 4:14; PSALM 139:13–16

⇢ PRAYER ⇠

Thank You for the call You've put on my life! Will You show me the next step I need to take to fulfill that call? Will You lead me and guide me on the path toward my destiny? Will You help me to release the gifts You've given me for Your glory?

SEE YOURSELF THROUGH THE EYES OF LOVE

*J*T'S TIME FOR you to see yourself the way I see you. When I look at you, I don't see you through the eyes of men. I see you through the eyes of love. I love you perfectly, so fear not and fret not over your imperfections. Do not look at or think about impossibilities.

See yourself as complete in Christ because that's how We see you. After you begin to see yourself the way We see you—and after you see Us in you— you will begin to manifest the maturity you desire and see the impossible become possible.

2 CORINTHIANS 6:17–18; 2 CORINTHIANS 5:21; COLOSSIANS 2:10

✦ PRAYER ✦

Open the eyes of my heart, Lord! Open my spiritual eyes to see myself as You see me and not as the world sees me or as I see myself. I set my heart to yield to Your work of forming Christ's character in me for His glory.

June 6

I Will Never Lead You Astray

Y OU'VE HESITATED. FEAR has held you back. Doubt has caused you to question My leading. I know you want complete assurance that you are heading in the right direction. But this is a walk of faith, a relationship of trust.

Trust your discernment. You can sense My promptings. Trust the Word. I will never lead you astray. Follow peace and refuse to move forward without it.

Faith is not science. It defies science. I will not let go of you. I will not let you fall when you walk in sincere faith. Do not be afraid.

ISAIAH 41:10; JAMES 1:6; HEBREWS 11:1

⟩ PRAYER ⟨

I refuse to listen to the voice of doubt any longer. I rebuke the voice of fear. I commit to following the peace that comes with Your leading. Help me to recognize and cast down vain imaginations that contradict Your Word.

Give Me Your Whole Heart

You've held a piece of yourself back—a piece of your heart. Lay your heart open before Me. I will not hurt you; I will heal you. Give Me your whole heart. Put your heart in My hands. Hold nothing back. Abandon yourself in Me. I know it's not comfortable, but as you set your heart toward My heart, I will comfort You. I will remove those things that hinder love. And when I take away the stumbling blocks erected in your soul, you will see My heart in a fresh way, and you will fully surrender to My will.

Proverbs 23:26; Romans 12:1; Matthew 7:21

→ Prayer ←

I surrender my will by the choice of my will. Not my will, Lord, but Yours be done. I refuse to hold anything back from You. I am Yours. You are mine. Show me what to do, and I will do it. Show me what not to do, and I will obey. Lead and guide me.

I Will Empower You to Overcome Sin

When I convict you of sin, I don't do it to make you feel guilty, condemned, or unworthy; I do it so that you can repent and receive Father's forgiveness. Repentance and forgiveness are among Our gifts to you. I do it so you can experience the cleansing power of the blood of Jesus, which removes the residue of unrighteousness and positions you to fellowship with Us in love. We love you! I will empower you to overcome sin if you ask Me.

PROVERBS 28:13; JAMES 4:8–10; REVELATION 3:19

→ PRAYER ←

Thank You that You have come to set the captives free. Thank You that You set me free even from my own desires that are contrary to Your perfect plan. Show me if there is any wicked way in me. By Your grace I will turn away from those things that hinder love.

PRACTICE MY PRESENCE IN EVERY SEASON

WHEN YOU FEEL the breeze blowing, think of Me. When you see the sun shining, think of Me. When you notice the raindrops falling, think of Me. Practice My presence in every season, and you will soon come to discern My moving in every situation.

You can't see Me, but you can know Me—and you can know that I am with you when the breeze is blowing, when the sun is shining, when the rain is falling—always. When you know I am with you, your confidence will soar.

ROMANS 1:18–21; PSALM 8:3–4; PSALM 19:1–6

✦ PRAYER ✦

I am so grateful that You are with me and that You will never leave me or forsake me—ever. But sometimes I forget the reality of Your ever-present help. Will You give me a greater sensitivity to You in every season and every situation?

ASK ME WHAT TO SAY AND
WHAT TO PRAY

*W*HEN YOU ARE at a loss for words, don't speak. Ask Me what you should say, and I will give you wisdom for every situation. Sometimes that wisdom is silence. Sometimes that wisdom is prayer.

When you don't have the words to pray, ask Me and I will help you. I will come alongside you and inspire your prayers. I will intercede to Father for you. I will pray a perfect prayer through you. I'm never at a loss for words, for prayers, or for anything you need. If I am silent, just wait in My presence. I have a plan, and I will reveal it to you.

LUKE 12:12; EXODUS 4:12; ROMANS 8:26

→ PRAYER ←

Sometimes I am too quick to speak. Help me to be quicker to listen than I am to make my voice heard. Teach me what to say and when to say it. Teach me what to pray and when to pray it. I won't speak about or move on a matter until I receive Your wisdom.

DISCERN WHAT I AM SAYING TO YOU THROUGH NATURAL THINGS

I WILL SPEAK TO you through the natural things around you—the people, the places, the things, and the circumstances. But be careful not to see every shifting wind as a prophetic instruction. As you fellowship with Me, you will learn to discern what I am saying to you through people, places, things, and circumstances—and also to know when something is trying to lead you away from My heart. Believe Me: when I speak, you will know it. When you are unsure, ask Me. I am trying not to hide truth from you but to reveal it.

PROVERBS 2:1–5; JOHN 10:27; 1 KINGS 19:11–12

⟶ PRAYER ⟵

Walking with You means walking in balance.
Teach me to recognize Your voice even in the
natural things, but guard my heart from making
assumptions and presumptions about Your will
as I walk through daily life. Show me the truth.

June 12

DON'T MOVE AHEAD
WITHOUT MY WISDOM

ISDOM CRIES ALOUD at every crossroad. Wisdom is not hiding in the shadows but is standing in the middle of your path to lead you into peace. Slow down. You don't have to answer now. You don't have to decide right now. Don't make a move until you hear wisdom's cries. Tune out all the other voices speaking into your situation and get alone with Me.

Cry out for wisdom, and wisdom will cry out to you. Cry out for understanding, and you will gain clarity. Don't move ahead without My wisdom. I long to share it with you! You'll know when you have it because it brings peace.

PROVERBS 1:20; JAMES 1:5; JAMES 3:17

✦ PRAYER ✦

*I am crying out to You right now for wisdom
and understanding. I am hungry for Your
peace. I need Your instruction in all my ways.
Thank You for Your faithfulness to lead me
and guide me into all truth one step at a time.*

Make More Room for My Presence

As I was with Jesus, so I am with you. I am available to you. You have access to My power. You can draw from My counsel. I will intercede for you. I will show you things to come. I will reveal Father's heart to you. I will advocate for you. I will anoint you to do everything Jesus has called you to do.

I am always here for you. The choice to receive all My blessings lies with you. What will you put away to make more room for My presence in your life? Together we can exalt Jesus in this generation. Are you willing?

John 16:13; 1 John 2:27; Galatians 5:24

☀ Prayer ☀

I've never had a friend like You. You are so committed to Me. I love You more than words can express. Help me to love You more. Help me to set aside activities that are not bearing fruit for Your kingdom so that I may press deeper into Your heart.

You Can't See the Future
If You're Looking Back

WHAT HAPPENED IN the past is past. It does not exist anymore except in your memory. It pains My heart to watch you meditate on things from the past that caused you pain. I have a future filled with hope for you. But you cannot see it as long as you are looking back. You will stumble over your past and delay the blessings Father has planned for your future if you do not let it go. So forgive and look up now, for Father has promised to vindicate those who trust in and wait on Him. He will do it.

JEREMIAH 29:11; ISAIAH 43:18; ROMANS 12:19

→ PRAYER ←

*Show me what I am holding on to that I
need to let go of, and I will choose this day
to let go, forgive, and refuse to look back on
it again. With Your help, I will no longer
recall bad memories. I will walk free into
the next stage of Your plan for my life.*

I Am With You Even When You Don't Sense My Presence

I KNOW THAT YOU love My presence, that you love to have an awareness of My presence. Please remember that I am with you even when you don't feel My presence. I never leave you; I am always with you.

If you want to feel My presence more, speak to Me. Begin sharing your heart with Me. Begin asking for My counsel. Begin thanking Me for what I'm doing in your life.

You will find that when your heart engages My heart with sincerity and simple faith, you will know that I abide in you even if you don't readily sense My presence. Know that I am with you.

John 14:16; 2 Corinthians 13:14; Jude 20

→ PRAYER ←

Yes, I love to feel Your presence, but I thank You that I am living not by feelings but by faith in the Word of God. Thank You for teaching me how to engage Your heart. Thank You for being willing to stand by my side through thick and thin.

June 16

DON'T STRETCH YOURSELF BEYOND MY GRACE

FATHER DOESN'T ALLOW more to come on you than you can bear. You are the one who takes on more than you can handle sometimes. Father will not call you to do more than He offers the grace to accomplish.

When you feel worn out and overwhelmed, you have stretched yourself beyond My grace. I'm calling you now into the place and the grace I've prepared for you. Remember, Jesus's yoke is easy and His burden is light. When you feel heavy and sense darkness encroaching, return to the place and grace I've prepared for you.

1 CORINTHIANS 10:13; 2 CORINTHIANS 12:9;
MATTHEW 11:30

→ PRAYER ←

Your words of life are true. Help me to remember them when I am tempted to take on more than I can bear—when my emotions tempt me to rush into something You haven't called me to. Help me to move in Your grace and not beyond it.

LOVE FOR LOVE'S SAKE

ᴸᴇᴛ ʏᴏᴜʀꜱᴇʟꜰ ɢᴏ. Lose yourself in Me. You will find yourself in My love. Love is the true measure of any man, any woman. I don't measure success by how much money you make or by how many people you impact or by how much you give to missions. At the end Jesus will judge your life on this earth by your love for people. Anything not motivated by love will be worthless in that day. Let Me teach you to love more. Let Me teach you to operate in love for love's sake, seeking nothing in return. By loving in this way, you will become like your beautiful Savior.

Jᴏʜɴ 13:34–35; Gᴀʟᴀᴛɪᴀɴꜱ 5:22–23; Rᴏᴍᴀɴꜱ 12:9–10

→ PRAYER ←

Yes, teach me to love. I know I fall short of perfect love in my relationships with other people. I repent right now for the times I have failed to walk in love. Shed Your love abroad in my heart once again and teach me to love.

YOUR HEART'S DESIRE IS TO RECEIVE LOVE

*Y*OUR DEEPEST HEART'S desire isn't really for more money or more status or more appreciation. Your deepest heart's desire is really to receive Our love and to return that love to Us. When you truly recognize this as your deepest desire and pursue it with everything in you, then Our peace will overtake you. Our joy will strengthen you. Our love will motivate you to lay down your life for the people around you. You won't be concerned about the money, the status, or the recognition—though they may come. You will be satisfied in Christ. This is Father's will for you.

JOHN 15:13; 1 JOHN 4:11; 1 JOHN 3:16–18

→ PRAYER ←

Help me to receive more of Your love. Enlarge
the capacity of my heart to drink in Your love.
Rid my heart of anything that gets in the way
of receiving Your love so I will have plenty of
Your love to give the people You put in my path.

Meet Me in the Secret Place

Will you meet Me in the secret place? It's just under the shadow of His wings. There you will find your fortress, your strong tower. It's a safe place where you are shielded from the warfare that tries to distract you from the beating of My heart and the words that I speak to you. Will you meet Me in that dwelling place? I am waiting for you there, to share wisdom and revelation in the knowledge of Jesus. Just close your eyes and ask Me to take you there now, and where I am you will be. I'm waiting....

Psalm 91; Psalm 90:1; Psalm 61:3

→ Prayer ←

You are my strong tower. You are my fortress. You are my dwelling place. You are my protection from the enemy. Draw me into Your presence—draw me closer to Your heart—and I will incline my ear to hear the words of life that will strengthen me.

YOUR PERSEVERING SPIRIT THRILLS MY HEART

ONE OF THE things I appreciate about you most is your perseverance. Some quit before they even get started—and you've had plenty of reasons to give up. The enemy has put many obstacles in your path. Man has put stumbling blocks in your way. But even when you fall down—even when life knocks you down—you don't stay down. A righteous person falls down seven times and gets back up again. I rejoice because you always get back up again. I love that about you.

JAMES 1:12; 2 TIMOTHY 2:12; HEBREWS 10:36

✦ PRAYER ✦

You have given me the ability to endure, to persevere, and to press on. Thank You for the strength to keep moving forward in Your will amid the opposition, the mistakes, the sin, and the weariness. I rejoice in You!

Draw Closer to Me

I WANT TO SHARE the secrets of the Father with you. Will you draw closer? When you learned about the still, small voice that spoke to Elijah, you were offered a principle in communicating with Me that too few truly understand: be still and know that Jesus is Lord.

Calm your mind. Draw near to Me, and I will draw near to you. The closer you draw to Me, the easier it will be to leave the distractions behind, still your soul, and hear Me whisper Father's secrets to your heart. Will you meet with Me now?

PSALM 25:14; PSALM 91:1; JAMES 4:8

→ PRAYER ←

Thank You for inviting me to meet with You. I accept! I will put away the distractions, quiet my soul, and wait on You. Teach me to be still—completely still—so I can hear Father's secrets from You.

June 22

REMEMBER THE JOY OF YOUR SALVATION

REMEMBER WHEN I revealed to you the Lamb of God who takes away the sin of the world? Remember when I showed you the truth about your Redeemer, King, and Bridegroom? Remember when you first accepted Jesus as your Lord and Savior? Now remember the joy you experienced—the joy of your salvation. That joy is the joy of the Lord. That joy is your strength. Don't let go of it! It will sustain you when you face a spiritual battle.

PSALM 51:12; NEHEMIAH 8:10; ISAIAH 12:2–3

→ PRAYER ←

I choose this day to enter into the joy of my salvation—a glorious joy that fills my heart with a desire to please You with every move I make, a joy that strengthens me. Help me to embrace that joy once again as I think about my First Love.

Do I Have Your Undivided Attention?

*Y*ou have My undivided attention, and there is no good thing I won't help you do. There is no righteous cause I've put on your heart that I won't help you pursue. There's no truth I won't lead you into. All I need is your undivided attention.

I want to show you Father's good plan for the next season so together we can cause His perfect will to come to pass in your life. I want to help you discern His righteous causes from man's fleshly works. I want to speak life-giving truth to your heart. You have My undivided attention. Do I have yours?

Hebrews 13:6; Hebrews 12:2; Malachi 3:18

✦ Prayer ✦

I am sorry for the times You've had to compete with the things of the world for my attention, and I set my heart to focus on You alone when You call me. I crave intimacy with You. You have my undivided attention.

REJECT THE VOICES OF
FEAR AND DOUBT

I SEE THAT FEAR sometimes distracts you from Father's best plans for you. We have told you over and over again to fear not, yet sometimes you still give ear to the fearful voices that seek to lead you away from your highest calling. I understand. I see your heart, and I hear the fearful thoughts—the thoughts of doubt—that bombard your mind. But I can do nothing to stop them.

Jesus gave you His authority, and your will dictates what you choose to think about. So think about Our love for you, and when you hear those fearful voices, reject them and embrace Our love.

ROMANS 8:38–39; PHILIPPIANS 4:8;
2 CORINTHIANS 10:5

✦ PRAYER ✦

I repent for heeding the voices of fear and doubt. Help me discern the subtle voices that try to tempt me to walk off Your perfect path. I commit to meditating on and walking in Your truth so I will be set free from the influences of fear and doubt.

I Am Speaking to You More Often Than You Realize

*A*RE YOU LISTENING? Really listening? I'm speaking to you more often than you realize. Those faint impressions, those deep knowings, those times scriptures seem to jump off the page, those small details of nature that catch your eye. I am speaking to you in and through many things.

I am hoping you'll speak back to My heart. I desire a holy conversation with you. Start watching. Start listening. Start waiting. Start observing. Start discerning. You'll soon become more sensitive to My ways of communicating.

JOHN 10:27; JEREMIAH 33:3; ROMANS 8:14

✦ PRAYER ✦

Even though I often hear Your voice, I know that You are speaking to me and leading me more times than I realize. I want to listen—really listen—to Your still, small voice. I want to engage in holy conversation with You. Please help me.

June 26

LET LOVE MOTIVATE YOUR WORDS AND ACTIONS

*T*AKE AN ETERNAL view on Earth—and act according to that eternal view—and it will change your life for eternity. The words you speak and the actions you take now have the potential to bring you eternal rewards. So be cautious not to speak idle words. Speak words that will edify, comfort, and exhort your brothers and sisters in Christ.

Use your words and actions to share the love of Christ with the lost ones around you. Whatever is not of faith is sin, but whatever is motivated by love has eternal impact. Take an eternal view, and let the love of God constrain you.

HEBREWS 13:14; COLOSSIANS 3:2; 1 PETER 1:3–4

→ PRAYER ←

*Help me to see things from a heavenly
perspective—and give me revelation and
understanding about the eternal impacts of
my decisions. Motivate my heart to share the
love of Christ. Help me to think thoughts of
love, speak words of love, and walk in love.*

GUARD YOUR HEART AGAINST DECEPTION

*J*UDGE NOT LEST you be judged. But know those who labor among you. Try the spirits to see if they are of God. Use the discernment I have given you. Sharpen your spiritual perception by being a student of the Word, for many false prophets have gone out into the world seeking to deceive the hearts of men. Gaze upon Jesus and you will be quicker to recognize the false workers, the false gospels, and the false doctrines. Guard your heart and know that Jesus is coming soon. Watch and pray.

MATTHEW 7:1; 1 THESSALONIANS 5:12;
LUKE 21:36

⤞ PRAYER ⤝

Help me to guard my heart. I don't want to be deceived by the wickedness rising up in this generation. Help me to keep my eyes firmly focused on Christ and to heed His Word so that I will discern the difference between truth and error.

June 28

Unlock the Power of My Covenant With You

When you said yes to Jesus, when you received Him as your Lord and Savior, you entered a covenant relationship that you did not understand. You still do not grasp the depth of Our everlasting covenant with you. We will never break the covenant, but you cannot receive the fullness of what it offers until you understand it more fully. Open the Scriptures and study about this covenant. As you do, I will pour out revelation and understanding that will unlock blessings.

Psalm 105:8; Hebrews 6:17–18; Matthew 26:28

✦ Prayer ✦

Thank You for Your covenant with me. You are not a covenant breaker but a covenant keeper. Please give me more understanding about the sacred covenant we have entered into. Give me revelation about the holy contract that binds us.

Put Me First in Your Life

WHEN YOU CHOOSE worship over enter-tainment, when you choose Scripture over a fiction novel, when you choose prayer over chatting with friends, it moves My heart. It really moves My heart. When you seek first the kingdom of God, you will find the kingdom of God and your Father who sits on the throne. You will find the King of kings and the Lord of lords.

Don't seek some supernatural encounter. Seek the kingdom, and you will find the supernatural. Choose worship. Choose Scripture. Choose prayer. Choose Us, for We have chosen you.

MATTHEW 6:33; DEUTERONOMY 4:29;
1 CORINTHIANS 13:11

✦ PRAYER ✦

I sense that You are calling me to put aside
childish things and enter into a new level
of Your glory, and I say yes to Your heart. I
say yes to Your will and yes to Your ways. I
say yes to worship and prayer. I say yes to
the supernatural life You want me to live.

June 30

SEEK MY BALANCE IN YOUR LIFE

SEEK MY BALANCE in all things. When I see you get out of balance in any area, it grieves Me because I know the enemy is looking for an opportunity to pounce.

Walking in the Word—being a doer of the Word—means setting boundaries. I am your safety net. I will always catch you. I will deliver you from the enemy's snare when you cry out to Me.

But I would much rather hear you crying out in intercession for another than pleading for rescue from the consequences of an imbalanced lifestyle. So seek balance in all things, and you will avoid many problems. You can close an open door to the enemy with a balanced life.

1 PETER 5:8; JAMES 1:22; MARK 6:31

→ PRAYER ←

I am being pulled in so many directions! Help me find the balance between serving and worshipping, between work and rest, between doing and being. Show me the changes I need to make in my life to shut the door to the enemy.

July

Now the works of the flesh are revealed, which are
these: adultery, sexual immorality, impurity, lewdness,
idolatry, sorcery, hatred, strife, jealousy, rage, selfish-
ness, dissensions, heresies, envy, murders, drunkenness,
carousing, and the like. I warn you, as I previously
warned you, that those who do such things shall not
inherit the kingdom of God. But the fruit of the Spirit
is love, joy, peace, patience, gentleness, goodness, faith,
meekness, and self-control; against such there is no law.

—GALATIANS 5:19–23

LEARN TO WAIT PATIENTLY

I KNOW PATIENCE HAS never been your strong point. I know it's not fun to wait for Father to move when you can so clearly see the path He has ordained for you. But patience can serve as protection—even a weapon in warfare. Patience will encourage you not to jump out ahead of My leading even when you can clearly see the next step. I see more than the next step and the end goal. I see the obstacles in between that will frustrate your progress if you are not spiritually prepared to overcome them. So be patient. Trust Me. We'll get there.

ROMANS 12:12; ROMANS 8:25; PSALM 37:7–9

✦ PRAYER ✦

*Patience is a fruit of the Spirit, so I ask You
to help me exhibit this fruit in my life. Help
me to cultivate it in my heart so that I
will not be troubled by what I see or don't
see. I commit myself to waiting on You.*

July 2

RECEIVE AND WALK IN MY LOVE

*Y*OU ARE WORTH everything to Me. You are My favorite! My love for you is so much greater than you know. I want to teach you how to receive My love in greater measure. I want to shed My love abroad in your heart more and more.

Love for you motivates Me. I want love for Me to motivate you in all that you do. I'm in this for love. I want you to be in this for love with Me.

When you begin to look at people and situations through the eyes of love, then you'll see them the way I do. Wisdom and compassion—and even miracles—will flow. Receive My love now, and pour it out on others. The world needs My love.

PSALM 139:13–16; EPHESIANS 2:4–9;
MATTHEW 6:25–34

→ PRAYER ←

I am overwhelmed by the knowledge of Your love for me. I know You love me. Yet I need a greater revelation of Your love in my heart. Help me see the world through the lens of Your love so that I can walk in supernatural love for people.

Are You Ready to Go Deeper in God?

*I*N DAYS OF old, before Jesus came to Earth, Father required many different sacrifices and vows and offerings from His people. Today He asks you to offer your whole heart to Him as a living sacrifice. In days of old there were strict systems in place to approach Him. Today He invites you to come boldly to His throne of grace to receive His mercy and find grace to help in times of need. In days of old worship was based on obedience and sometimes fear. Today Father wants you to worship Him in spirit and truth with a sincere heart of love. Are you ready to go deeper?

ROMANS 12:1; HEBREWS 4:16; JOHN 4:24

❖ PRAYER ❖

Yes, I'm ready to go deeper, but I can't do it without Your help. Help me present my body to Father as a living sacrifice. Help me approach His throne of grace boldly. Help me to worship Him in spirit and in truth. I am ready, but I need Your help.

July 4

WE'RE IN THIS TOGETHER

*W*E'RE IN THIS together. We are co-laborers. I'll never leave you alone in the battle to establish God's will in the earth. I'll always lead you on the best possible path, even if it means taking you on a long journey through the wilderness; even if it means leading you through spiritual warfare; even it means hiding Myself from you so that you feel as if you can't sense My presence or hear My voice. I'm committed to you. I'm dedicated to you. We're in this together. Never think anything different. I am here to stay. You have My word. I love you.

1 CORINTHIANS 3:9; 2 CORINTHIANS 6:1;
HEBREWS 6:13–20

✢ PRAYER ✢

Thank You for counting me worthy to serve as an ambassador for Christ, a co-laborer in Your kingdom, and for giving me the strength to walk on the path You've designed for me despite the resistance. Help me to walk in Your perfect will.

My Grace Is Sufficient

*I*T'S GRIEVOUS TO watch you get frustrated by the enemy's tactics, by the undesirable circumstances in life, and by people who set out to provoke you. It's grievous because you cannot receive My grace to overcome and walk in love when you allow frustration to rule in your soul. My grace is sufficient for you. Indeed, I am the Spirit of grace.

My grace is available to you, but you have to position yourself to receive it. Frustration puts up a wall that hinders you from receiving My grace. So stay peaceful and talk to Me about what's bothering you. Don't give in to frustration. We'll work it out together.

2 CORINTHIANS 12:9; JOHN 1:16; 2 TIMOTHY 4:22

❖ PRAYER ❖

Thank You for Your grace, and thank You that it is sufficient for me in every situation. Thank You that Your power is made perfect in weakness. Help me to position my heart to receive Your abundant grace and reject the feelings of frustration that open the door to the enemy.

July 6

SEEK MY MIND ON EVERY MATTER

ES, THERE IS wisdom in the counsel of many. But be careful not to draw on the world's wisdom. I inspired David to write these words: "Blessed is the man who walks not in the counsel of the ungodly." It's OK to seek advice from wise, godly counselors, but that's no guarantee they have My mind on a matter.

Remember this: My wisdom is pure, peaceable, gentle, and reasonable. My wisdom is full of mercy and good fruits. It doesn't waver, and there's no hypocrisy in it. Meditate on these truths and you will quickly learn to recognize My wisdom in every situation.

PROVERBS 15:22; PSALM 1:1; JAMES 3:17

→ PRAYER ←

I don't want to hear or heed any wisdom that is not springing from Your heart. Surround me with godly counselors, and give me an ear to hear Your voice in their words. Speak Your wisdom directly to my heart, and I will walk in Your ways.

Open Your Heart to Father

I KNOW MANY HAVE portrayed Father as a harsh monarch who is holier-than-thou. He *is* holy—perfectly holy—but you should not shrink back from His heart in your humanity. The enemy has lied about Father for ages because He doesn't want people to draw close to Him. He is holy, but He is also merciful. He is for you, not against you. He desires relationship over religious rules.

Father loves you the same way He loves Jesus. Think about that! Even though you are not yet perfected, you are perfectly loved. So fear not, but open your heart fully to your Father in heaven who loves you. When you see Him the way He truly is, your soul will take comfort in His great mercy and love.

LUKE 6:36; ROMANS 8:31; ROMANS 5:8

→ PRAYER ←

Help me to be holy even as my Father in heaven is holy. I want to see Him as He is because He sees me as I am. I want to love Him the way Jesus does because He loves me the way He loves Jesus. Thank You for Your great love and mercy for me.

July 8

BLESS THOSE WHO CURSE YOU

WHEN PEOPLE PERSECUTE you for Jesus's sake, turn the anger you feel into prayer power. Instead of stewing over the negative words they are speaking against you, break the word curses by the authority of your King and launch into prayer. Launch into prayer for your persecutors.

Bless those who curse you. Bless and curse not. Move in the spirit opposite to the spirit that's moving against you. Then you will truly be like Christ. You will manifest His love for your enemies, and your anointed prayers may set them free.

MATTHEW 5:44; LUKE 6:28; ROMANS 12:20

→ PRAYER ←

I want to be like Christ, even when people speak nasty words about me and to me. I want to be like my Father in heaven, returning good for evil over and over. Help me to show Your love to people who are not showing Your love to me.

People Are Not Your Enemies

*Y*ou need to always remember this: you are not wrestling against flesh and blood. The people around you who are making your life difficult or talking behind your back are not your enemies. No, many times there are unseen forces influencing them. Many times they are acting out of hurts and wounds from the pasts or insecurities from the present. Many times they are giving way to the enemy's plan and following the urges of the carnal nature.

You are not battling flesh and blood but principalities, powers, and spiritual wickedness in high places and demonic forces in low places. Rise above the battle in Christ.

Ephesians 6:12; Luke 8:27–30; 1 Peter 3:9

✦ Prayer ✦

Help me see people the way You do. Show me why they are lashing out against me or others so that I can be an agent of healing and peacemaking. Help me to hold my tongue and to treat others the way I want to be treated even when they are unkind to me.

July 10

YOU MUST DISCERN THE ENEMY

*Y*OU CAN'T BIND a strongman you don't see. You can't bind a devil you are unable to discern. You can't win a battle against an enemy you aren't engaging. Sometimes you think you know what the enemy's assignment against you is based on past experience, and sometimes you are right. But deduction based on experience is different from discernment that you receive from Me.

You have positional victory in battle through Christ, but you need discernment to carry out My battle plans. Stop and ask Me, and I will reveal the enemy that is coming against you and give you the strategy to counter the attack.

MARK 3:27; MATTHEW 16:19;
1 CORINTHIANS 12:7–10

✦ PRAYER ✦

Help me to move in discernment and not in presumption, assumption, or deduction. I need revelation from You to truly know what I am up against and what is up against me. Sharpen my discernment so that I am able to bind the strongman.

YOU CAN OVERCOME
LIFE'S DISTRACTIONS

HERE WILL ALWAYS be distractions around you. You can never rid yourself of all the distractions in this life. The only way to overcome the distractions is to refuse to give them your eyes, your ears, your mouth, and your mind. In other words, stop thinking about them! Stop listening. Stop looking. Stop talking about them. There is tremendous power in a life focused singularly on Jesus and His will—tremendous power. The decision is yours.

PROVERBS 20:12; PSALM 119:15; PROVERBS 5:1

⚘ PRAYER ⚘

*Distractions rise up against me every day, but
I refuse to give them my eyes, my ears, or my
mouth any longer. Help me to think according to
the mind of Christ so they will not enter my mind
either. Set a guard over my mouth and cause
me to speak according to what You teach me.*

July 12

I Am Here When You Need Me

*P*EOPLE—BOTH FRIENDS AND enemies— will come and go. But I will remain with you. When friends move on, I will be with you. When enemies rise up and attack, I will be with you. When you feel as if all is lost, as if no one understands, I will be with you. When it seems as if all hell is breaking loose against you, I assure you that I am with you. Jesus sent Me to abide in you. I am here when you need Me. I am always right here.

JOSHUA 1:9; 1 CORINTHIANS 3:16; PSALM 139:10

⁂ PRAYER ⁂

*I am so grateful that You abide in me and
I abide in You! I am so thankful that You
will never leave me or forsake me! You dwell
in my heart through faith, so I need not
fear or be discouraged. Give me a greater
revelation of Your presence in my life.*

ASK, AND YOU WILL RECEIVE

*Y*OU HAVE NOT because you ask not. When you ask with pure motives for what Father already desires to give you, you'll get what you ask for. When you follow My leading—when you ask for what I prompt your heart to petition—you will have what you ask for. It's really that simple. If you aren't making your requests known—if you aren't asking—you will not receive all We have for you.

Sometimes you don't ask either because you think you can't get it or because you are afraid you won't. Change the way you think. Ask for what you believe is Father's will. Follow My leading. You'll see answers to prayer begin to flow as you follow My lead.

JAMES 4:3; PHILIPPIANS 4:6; 1 JOHN 5:14

→ PRAYER ←

Thank You for encouraging me to ask. I will ask with confidence, knowing that if I ask anything according to Your will, You will hear and answer me. Help me to hold steadfast to Your promises even when I don't see an immediate answer.

July 14

FOCUS ON THE SOLUTION, NOT THE OBSTACLE

When you face an obstacle of any kind, you have two clear choices: focus on the obstacle and get frustrated with the one you believe put it there, or focus on the solution and the One who has the wisdom to help you overcome the obstacle. There will always be obstacles, and if you focus too much on them, you'll become discouraged. See the obstacles—but then turn to the One who has the wisdom and strategy that will lead you into victory. Only you control what you focus on.

MATTHEW 17:20; ISAIAH 57:14; JOHN 16:33

→ PRAYER ←

I choose this day to see the obstacles in my path but not to allow them to discourage me from moving forward in Your will. I will not meditate on the obstacles and challenges. I will meditate on Jesus, the author and finisher of my faith.

I Am Changing You

*I*KNOW THAT YOU see in part and know in part where I want to take you, and you realize it's good. You want to get to that place in Christ now. You want to be more like Him—right now. But be assured, know, and believe that I am changing you from glory to glory. Be patient with yourself and be patient with the process. We are patient with you.

I am transforming you into the image of Christ little by little. Your job is to spend time with Me, spend time in the Word—and believe. Only believe. You can't change yourself, but be assured, know, and believe: I am doing it.

1 CORINTHIANS 13:9; 2 CORINTHIANS 3:18;
ROMANS 8:29

→ PRAYER ←

I've tried and failed to change myself. I can't do it. I choose now to yield to Your work in my life. You are so patient and kind. I surrender my heart to You and ask You to take me from glory to glory as I fellowship with You and meditate on Your Word.

July 16

I Want to Teach You About My Love

I WANT TO TEACH you about My love. I want you to know the depth of My love, to see the length of My love, to experience the height of My love, to walk in the width of My love. I want you to learn to love others the way I love you. Will you let Me teach you?

It all starts with learning to receive My love, and that means rooting out religious mind-sets about who Father is, who Jesus is, and who I am. I am love. In the end of this age love is what will measure your heart. Love never fails.

EPHESIANS 3:14–19; 1 CORINTHIANS 13:4–8; LUKE 10:27

→ PRAYER ←

I want to go with You on this love journey. I want to move deeper into Your love. Take me where You want me to go so that I am able to not only receive what You have for me but also show others the way to Your heart. Teach me to love You and to love others as You do.

REFUSE TO ACCEPT PRESSURE FROM THE WORLD

*T*HE PRESSURE YOU often feel in your daily walk is not coming from Us. The world will pressure you. The world will guilt you. The world will stretch you to your breaking point. The world will violate your boundaries. The world will use you and abuse you—if you let it. But Jesus's yoke is easy and His burden is light.

I will lead you to prefer others. I will lead you to deny self. I will lead you to love. I will lead you to pick up your cross and follow Christ. But I will not pressure you or condemn you or guilt you or shame you as the world does. Seek to please Father, and don't receive pressure from man or devils. Follow Me.

1 JOHN 5:19; 1 CORINTHIANS 2:12;
1 THESSALONIANS 4:1–2

→ PRAYER ←

I refuse the pressure, the guilt, and the stress the world brings. I will not bow down to the spirit of this world, which offers nothing good. I will bow down to the Spirit of God. Help me resist the devil and follow You in all my ways.

Be Quick to Listen, Slow to Speak, and Slow to Anger

WHY DO YOU think I warned you to be quick to listen, slow to speak, and slow to anger? Because by being quick to listen, you remain teachable. You also give yourself more opportunity to discern the spirit behind the words you hear. By being slow to speak, you avoid saying anything rash or using words that lack My wisdom. By being slow to anger, you avoid silly arguments over petty matters. Take time to really listen and take time to respond. Don't let the enemy provoke you.

JAMES 1:19; PROVERBS 15:31; PROVERBS 1:5

→ PRAYER ←

I commit myself to being slow to speak and quick to listen. Help me discern the spirit behind the words that are spoken in my hearing so that I will not fall into the enemy's trap. Holy Spirit, give me ears to hear what You are saying at all times.

YOUR WORDS HAVE POWER

*I*F YOU TRULY understood the power of your words, you would speak differently. Father spoke things into existence, and you can do the same. You can frame the world with the words of your mouth.

The power of life and death are in your tongue. I know you have heard this many, many times before, but have you *really* heard? I want you to receive revelation and understanding about this life-changing principle. It is a spiritually discerned truth. Do you want this revelation? I'm here to show you.

PROVERBS 18:21; MATTHEW 12:36–37; PROVERBS 13:3; 1 PETER 3:10

✦ PRAYER ✦

I've read so many times about the power of words, yet I still fail to measure mine. Put a coal to my lips as You did to Isaiah's. Teach me to speak in line with Your truth. Set a guard over my mouth. Give me a revelation of the power of words.

July 20

CONSIDER WHAT YOU'RE THINKING ABOUT

SOMETIMES YOU AREN'T quick enough to catch your thoughts—those vain imaginations that exalt themselves against the knowledge of Christ. Sometimes you don't discern them and cast them down fast enough. Sometimes you meditate on them without even realizing it. Sometimes you fall into this demonic trap.

But consider your emotions. Your emotions are influenced by your thoughts. So when you find that your emotions are out of line with peace, joy, and love, stop and consider your thoughts. Then cast down the offenders and replace them with the truth.

2 CORINTHIANS 10:5; GALATIANS 5:22–23;
HEBREWS 10:23

✦ PRAYER ✦

Help me manifest the fruit of self-control when my emotions try to take me out of the spirit and into the flesh. Give me spiritual ears to hear the thoughts the enemy speaks, and give me the boldness to rise up with the sword of the Spirit.

Live With Eternity in Mind

$\mathcal{A}$RE YOU READY for the return of Jesus? Are you prepared for His Second Coming? Are you living every day as if He may come back at any time? I know the answers to those questions. I want you to search your soul and see where you stand in light of eternity. Your salvation is secure, but eternity is about more than your salvation. Your obedience to complete your God-given assignments in this age will impact the rewards you receive in the age to come. It's never too late to be more obedient. Live your life with eternity in mind.

LUKE 18:8; MATTHEW 24:43–44;
MATTHEW 25:21

→ PRAYER ←

Give me the grace of obedience. Give me a watchful eye. Give me an eternal perspective. Give me the diligence to watch and pray because when Jesus returns, I want to be declared a good and faithful servant.

JUST SURRENDER

I KNOW SOMETIMES YOU feel like giving up. But don't give up. No, don't give up. Instead, surrender. Don't bow to the enemy's pressure to quit. Surrender fully—with all that you are and all that you have—to Father's will. Surrender to His perfect plan. Surrender to His Word. Surrender to His ways. Just surrender.

Say it now: "I surrender." Surrender brings freedom and delivers you from the temptation to quit and give up. Abandon yourself to Father wholeheartedly and don't look back.

MATTHEW 16:24–27; ROMANS 12:1;
LUKE 9:57–62

→ PRAYER ←

I refuse to give up, and I resolve to surrender. Let me experience the freedom of total surrender to Your will. Help me remain steadfast in my surrender to Your ways. Make me willing in the day of Your power.

Come Away With Me

Come away with Me. Leave behind the distractions and frustrations and even the daily routine—just for a little while. Come away with Me. Set yourself apart for a few hours. I want to talk with you. I want to touch your heart. I want to listen to you. I want to teach you. I want to reveal to you things to come. I want to strengthen you. I want to comfort you. I want to give you strategies to overcome the distractions and frustrations. Come away with Me for a little while. I want to refresh you.

Psalm 23:3; Exodus 15:2; Psalm 29:11

→ Prayer ←

I dedicate myself to You. I cast my cares on You. I yield myself to You. Speak to my heart and refresh my soul. Hear my cries and teach me the way I should go. Pour Yourself out on me, and strengthen my resolve to obey Your leading.

WALK HAND IN HAND WITH ME

As we walk together hand in hand, heart to heart, know that I will never let you go. I will never lose My hold on you. I have you. But sometimes you let go of My hand. Sometimes you disconnect from My heart. Sometimes you run ahead of My leading, and sometimes you lag behind when I am trying to take you somewhere new. Even then, you are on My heart and in My sight. Even then, I am waiting and watching and calling out. So when you feel as if I am not walking beside you, look around because I am still here. I am just not as close as I'd like to be. Walk with Me.

PSALM 119:105; MICAH 6:8; GALATIANS 5:16

✦ PRAYER ✦

Thank You that You are a friend who sticks closer than a brother. Forgive me for the times I have walked ahead of You or behind You, and give me a sensitivity to You that will help me walk in lockstep with You.

EXPECT MORE FROM ME

*K*NOW IT SOMETIMES feels as if people expect a lot from you—more than you feel you can give, more than you should have to give, more than they are willing themselves to give. I know it sometimes feels as if people are pulling you in a million different directions with no consideration for your boundaries. People will always expect more from you than you can give.

As for you, stop expecting so much from other people, and start expecting more from Me. When you do, you will not be disappointed. I will give you the grace to do everything I've called you to do.

MATTHEW 6:15; ISAIAH 30:18;
2 CORINTHIANS 9:8

⇥ PRAYER ⇤

Those who trust in the Lord will never be disappointed. I choose this day to trust in You for the grace I need to rise up and handle everything You expect me to do—and for the courage to say no to those things You have not called me to do.

July 26

KEEP A HEAVENLY PERSPECTIVE

ET YOUR MIND on things in heaven and not on things of Earth. Everything on Earth will fade away. All your problems, all your fears, all your "things" are only temporary.

You will have less trouble with your troubles and experience less fear if you keep a heavenly perspective. Keep Father's perspective on your trials and tribulations. Then you will have the confidence and peace you need to move through them even as you move toward your eternal rewards.

COLOSSIANS 3:1–2; ISAIAH 40:4–8; 1 PETER 5:10

→ PRAYER ←

Life is filled with distractions. Nevertheless, I choose to set my mind on things above and not on the things of this world. Help me to maintain a heavenly perspective and to reject the fears and worries the world tries to bring to my heart.

I Can Help You Find Rest

*T*HE ENEMY'S JOB is to weary the saints. I see your weariness. I see your worries. But I also see your thirst. I see your hunger for righteousness. Jesus invited all those who are weary and heavy-laden to come to Him, and He promised to provide rest. Take His yoke upon you and let Him teach you because He is gentle and humble of heart. You will find rest for your soul.

I can show you how to find that rest for your soul. I can teach you about Jesus, your Prince of Peace. Weariness will leave when you see Jesus as He is and understand His love for you. Let Me show you.

REVELATION 13:7; MATTHEW 11:28–30; ISAIAH 9:6

→ PRAYER ←

I believe that You can show me how to find rest for my soul. Teach me how to overcome the spirit of weariness that comes against me. Teach me more about the rest Christ promised me. Show me Jesus as He is, and I will not grow weary in well doing.

July 28

I Want to Fill You to Overflowing

I want to fill you with more of Me. Do you want more? Will you yield to Me? I want to fill you to overflowing so that you will be a strong witness that Jesus is alive. I want to fill you to overflowing so that My supernatural gifts will manifest through you. I want to fill you with more of Me.

I see your thirst and I can satisfy it. Your part is to drink deeply of Me. Receive My fullness and all that I bring with Me.

EPHESIANS 5:18; JOHN 7:38; ACTS 1:8

→ PRAYER ←

Yes, I want more of You. Yes, I will yield to You. I want to be a witness for Christ in this generation. I want to move in Your supernatural gifts. I want to drink deeply of You. Fill me again so that I may overflow with Your love.

As You Depend on Me, You Will Move in a Greater Anointing

*A*s you learn to depend more on Me and less on yourself, you will move in a greater anointing because I will pour out My grace on you to meet every task and tackle every challenge. When you begin depending more and more on Me and less and less on other people, you will receive more and more wisdom, revelation, and understanding directly from My heart to yours. I am dependable. You can depend on Me. Let Me meet you where you are and meet your every need.

John 3:30; 2 Corinthians 12:9; Zechariah 4:6

→ Prayer ←

I refuse to depend on the arm of flesh—or the wisdom of man. It's not by might, nor by power, but by You, the Spirit of God, that I will overcome, endure, and prosper. Help me to resist the temptation to lead and to depend on my natural abilities instead of on You.

July 30

THE BEST IS YET TO COME

REMEMBER HOW FAR We have brought you. Remember how much you have changed. Didn't We deliver you from every trial? Didn't We show you the way of escape? Didn't We bring increase through the pain and those things you willingly—and not so willingly—left behind to follow Us? Didn't We tell you better things were ahead? Weren't We right?

And now, I tell you that your latter will be greater than your past. Yes, the best is yet to come. Get ready.

2 CORINTHIANS 1:10; JOHN 16:13; 1 JOHN 3:2

→ PRAYER ←

Thank You for changing me from glory to glory. You have restored my soul and renewed my mind. You are faithful. Please help me now to prepare myself for what You have planned for me next. Help me ready my heart to follow You.

COME WITH ME TO A SECRET PLACE

I WILL MEET YOU where you are if you'll let Me lead you where I want to take you. For I have a place in mind—a place in Me—where I desire to fellowship with you in a deeper way. It's a secret place, a place you haven't been before. It's a place of worship where Our hearts will connect with yours in a fresh way. It's a place where you will forget all those things that distract you from Our love and remember those things We've shared with you in days past.

It's been a while. I'll meet you where you are. Will you come with Me?

ROMANS 8:14; JOHN 4:24; 2 CORINTHIANS 13:14

✦ PRAYER ✦

Yes, I will go anywhere with You. Lead me and guide me into the secret place, into a place of worship, into a place of intimacy with You. Help me make a heart connection that will forever change me. I am ready.

August

There is therefore now no condemnation for those who are in Christ Jesus, who walk not according to the flesh, but according to the Spirit. For the law of the Spirit of life in Christ Jesus has set me free from the law of sin and death. For what the law could not do, in that it was weak through the flesh, God did by sending His own Son in the likeness of sinful flesh, and concerning sin, He condemned sin in the flesh, in order that the righteous requirement of the law might be fulfilled in us, who walk not according to the flesh but according to the Spirit. For those who live according to the flesh set their minds on the things of the flesh, but those who live according to the Spirit, the things of the Spirit.

—ROMANS 8:1–5

I Will Tell You What You Need to Know

*I*F YOU COULD figure out everything yourself, you wouldn't need Me, would you? Although you have intelligence and the ability to reason, you can't see the end from the beginning, can you? You can't see what goes on in the spiritual realm for good or bad unless I show you. You can't see what's just around the next corner in your life unless I reveal it. You have intelligence and reasoning, but I have wisdom and revelation. I am willing and ready to share with you what you need to know if you will ask and listen.

EPHESIANS 1:17; PSALM 119:18; JOHN 16:13

◆ PRAYER ◆

You're right; I can't figure it all out. I need You! Open my eyes so I can see what You are trying to show me. Give me a spirit of wisdom and revelation in the knowledge of Christ. Lead me into all truth. I am asking and listening.

August 2

PARTNER WITH ME IN PRAYER

ℙARTNERING WITH ME in prayer does more than pave the way for the answers, and it does more than change your circumstances; it changes your heart and mind. You cannot connect with Me in prayer without fellowshipping with Me in the process. And when you partner with Me in prayer, you rely on My leading to pray the perfect prayer. You lean not on your own understanding. You allow Me to direct your prayers to Father. We come into unity to bring Father's will into your life. That thrills Me.

ROMANS 8:26–27; EPHESIANS 6:18; JUDE 20

→ PRAYER ←

Thank You for interceding for me according to Father's will. As I pray with my spirit and my mind, help me petition Father rightly. Will You come alongside me and help me make my requests known to Him even when I don't know what to pray?

See Christ's Glory

When you truly see the glory of the Lamb of God who took away your sins, you will begin to relate to Him differently. You will begin to receive from Father more freely those things you need to accomplish His will, whether provision or healing or wisdom or anything else. When you truly see the glory of the Lamb of God who took away your sins, you will walk in a liberty and a confidence that attracts people to Jesus for the salvation of their souls. Meditate on the glory of the Lamb of God who took away your sins and established you securely as an ambassador in His kingdom.

John 1:29; 2 Timothy 2:8; Hebrews 1:3–4; Colossians 1:16–20

→ Prayer ←

Holy Spirit, I want to see Jesus the way You do. I want to see Him in His power and majesty. I want to see His glory. Reveal to me the nature and character of Christ so that the truth about who He is and who I am in Him will set me free.

August 4

SPEND MORE TIME WITH ME

*Y*OU'LL NEED TO make adjustments in your schedule to fulfill My highest call on your life. Yes, a change in the way you spend your time is required to reach your destiny. You pray, but you must extend your prayer time. You worship, but you must press in a little deeper. You study, but there's so much more I want to show you! If you'll commit to spending thirty minutes more with Me in the evenings, even though you are tired, I will bring rest, restoration, refreshing, revelation, and still more blessings to your spirit, soul, and body. I want to spend more time with you. You know where to find Me.

EPHESIANS 5:16; MATTHEW 6:33; JOHN 15:1–5

✦ PRAYER ✦

Show me the changes I need to make in my life to pursue more of You. Help me to set aside any weight that's slowing me down as I run my race in Christ. Draw me into prayer, and give me a hunger for Your Word. Help me to obey You.

DON'T MEDITATE ON YOUR MISTAKES

ATHER'S MERCIES ARE new every morning, so don't start your day meditating on the mistakes you made yesterday. When you repent, you are restored to perfect fellowship with Father that empowers you to live a holy life. Meditating on the mistakes of yesterday sets you up to make the same mistakes today.

What you focus on is what will draw your soul. What you meditate on will produce fruit, either good or bad. So instead of meditating on your sins unto condemnation, meditate on Father's forgiveness unto cleansing. Then ask for grace to walk in holiness.

LAMENTATIONS 3:22–23; 1 JOHN 1:9;
PSALM 51:2–4

→ PRAYER ←

Thank You for Your great mercy toward me. Help me to receive Your mercy and Your forgiveness so that I will walk free in the newness of life Jesus offers me. Help me not to make the same mistakes again. Pour out Your grace to walk in holiness.

August 6

GIVE THANKS ALWAYS

*W*HEN YOU ARE tempted to complain, find something to thank Us for instead. Complaining is a temptation the enemy brings. But remember that the power of life and death is in your tongue. When you complain, you are speaking death over a thing.

Instead of voicing your dissatisfaction, thank Me for the wisdom to overcome what's frustrating you, to solve the problems that face you, to confront the enemy with the sword of the Spirit, or to walk away from a situation and let Me handle it. Your praise empowers you to focus on receiving My wisdom and speaking life—even to those things that smell of death.

PHILIPPIANS 2:14–16; EPHESIANS 5:20;
1 THESSALONIANS 5:18

✦ PRAYER ✦

Help me to maintain a grateful heart in the midst of frustrating circumstances, trials, enemy attacks, and bad days. I will no longer complain but will lift my voice in praise and thanksgiving to the One who gives me strength and wisdom to overcome.

KEEP YOUR EYES ON JESUS

*D*IDN'T I TELL you I'd work everything out for good? Didn't I express My will to your heart? Aren't all My promises yes and amen? The enemy tries to rob you of your faith, wear you out, and burn you out by showing you all the things that could go wrong. He tries to steal your peace by bringing difficult people into your life who oppose Father's will. Shut your natural eyes, seal your lips, and look on Jesus. He will deliver you from the narrow straits and take you into a broad place.

ROMANS 8:28; 2 CORINTHIANS 1:20;
EPHESIANS 6:16

✦ PRAYER ✦

*Thank You for reminding me of Your
Word. I choose to walk in faith. I choose
to lift up my shield of faith and quench all
the flaming darts of the enemy. Help me
to keep my eyes off my circumstances and
on the Author and Finisher of my faith.*

August 8

You Have Authority Over the Enemy

*Y*ou overcome by the blood of Jesus and the word of your testimony—and by denying yourself no matter what the cost as you pursue Father's will. These are spiritual warfare principles. Walk in these principles, and you will manifest the victory that belongs to you in Christ.

You have authority over the enemy in the name of Jesus because you have accepted the work of the Cross. Declare your authority and remain willing to continue decreasing so He will increase—and the devil will surely flee.

Revelation 12:11; Luke 9:23; James 4:7

→ Prayer ←

Thank You for the blood of the Lamb! Help me to crucify my flesh. Help me to deny myself. Help me to pick up my cross and follow Christ anywhere and everywhere. I declare that I have authority over the enemy in Jesus's name. Please give me a greater understanding of this authority.

KNOW PEOPLE BY THE SPIRIT

PEOPLE DON'T ALWAYS prove trustworthy—
even those who call themselves Christians—
but you can always trust the Christ who created
them. When you enter into new relationships, be
discerning but not suspicious. Believe the best and
know them by the spirit rather than by the flesh.

Remember, Samuel thought Eliab was the best
choice for the next king of Israel, but the Lord
looks on the heart. Ask Father to show you the
heart of the person and His heart for them, and it
will change your relationship dynamics. And as far
as it depends on you, be trustworthy.

1 SAMUEL 16:7; JOHN 15:12; LUKE 6:32

→ PRAYER ←

*You are trustworthy even when people are not
trustworthy. Give me a discerning heart so I
can enter into new friendships with those You've
called me to befriend. And above all, help me
show Christ's love even when it is not returned.*

August 10

ALWAYS BELIEVE THE BEST

DON'T THINK THE worst. Believe the best. It's up to you. The enemy has only negative thoughts to share; My thoughts toward you are positive. The enemy's thoughts toward you are condemning; My thoughts toward you are loving. The enemy's thoughts toward you are for evil; My thoughts toward you are pure and for good.

Call upon Me. Come and pray with Me. I will help you cast down the enemy's negative, condemning, evil thoughts and share My way of thinking with you.

JEREMIAH 29:11; JOHN 10:10; PSALM 139:17–18

→ PRAYER ←

I put on the helmet of salvation right now and choose to believe the best—to believe what Your Word says about every situation. Help me to reject the thoughts of the enemy and embrace Your thoughts about me so I will see myself the way You do.

MY SPIRIT OF PEACE ABIDES IN YOU

*E*VEN WHEN CHAOS surrounds you, peace abides within you. Jesus left you His peace, and He is the Prince of Peace. I am the Spirit of peace. You may be facing unpleasant circumstances and have difficult people in your path. But that does not change the reality that Jesus left you His peace and I, the Spirit of peace, abide in you. So it's up to you. You can focus on the chaos of the world, or you can focus on My peace. I won't help you focus on chaos, but I will help you overcome it by teaching you how to remain peaceful.

ISAIAH 9:6; 2 THESSALONIANS 3:16; ISAIAH 55:12

✢ PRAYER ✢

Thank You for Your peace. Help me to appropriate Your peace even in the midst of a storm. Give me the determination to go after peace in every situation. Give me a craving for peace, and give me the grace to be a maker and maintainer of peace.

Learn the Art of Casting

Study the word *cast* and you'll better understand the good fight of faith. When you cast your cares upon Jesus, when you cast down vain imaginations and high things that exalt themselves against the knowledge of God, when you cast out demons—you are taking strong action. But to "cast" requires effort. The cares, imaginations, and demons do not go willingly. You have to purposely and aggressively cast those things away. It's part of the battle. Embrace the art of casting, and you will manifest great victories.

1 Peter 5:7; 2 Corinthians 10:5; Matthew 10:1

✦ Prayer ✦

Teach me the art of casting as I commit to understanding this spiritual warfare concept. When the enemy casts cares, imaginations, and oppression upon me, show me how to cast these things off and refuse to receive them again.

GOD TRULY UNDERSTANDS YOU

$\mathcal{S}$OME PEOPLE WON'T understand you. In fact, they will misunderstand you. Being misunderstood may cause pain in your soul, but remember that Jesus was misunderstood, mistreated, and maligned. You, My friend, are in good company. Father has been misunderstood greatly, and many have misjudged His heart for those He created. I too am widely misunderstood and even ignored. When people misunderstand you, don't take it to heart. We understand you completely. We love you just as you are.

MARK 3:21; MATTHEW 12:22–30; HEBREWS 4:15

→ PRAYER ←

I'm so grateful that I have a Comforter who understands and can empathize with my quirks, my weaknesses, and my disappointments. Please help me to lean into You when I feel the pain of being misunderstood so You can comfort me.

August 14

I Will Reveal Mysteries

I WANT TO SHOW you the mysteries of the kingdom. I want to share with you things eye has not seen nor ear heard nor mind conceived. I want to show you what Father has prepared for you, the one He loves so deeply. It is within My power to reveal these things.

I have searched Father's heart and discovered treasures reserved just for you. I will reveal them to you little by little as you walk with Me. I will reveal mysteries to you.

MATTHEW 13:11; 1 CORINTHIANS 2:9; ISAIAH 45:3

✦ PRAYER ✦

I want to know the mysteries. I want to see those unseen things Father has prepared for me. Quicken my heart to walk with You and talk with You throughout the day so I don't miss anything You are trying to reveal to me.

I Will Lead You to the Truth

$\mathcal{M}$ANY TIMES IT'S better to say nothing to people about the challenges you face and the roadblocks that stand in the way between you and My revealed will. Many do not have My mind on the matter, and many, though well-meaning, will offer advice that is not based on My wisdom.

I am the Spirit of truth. I will lead you and guide you into the truth you need. I am not trying to hide the truth from you. Seek My wisdom about the challenges and roadblocks. Assuredly, I will show you the truth that sets you free.

PROVERBS 17:18; EXODUS 14:14; PROVERBS 29:11

✦ PRAYER ✦

I will quietly wait for You at all times because You are the One who delivers me from every snare. Help me to be still before You and wait patiently on You. Help me to guard my mouth and restrain my lips from discussing with others what it is better not to share. Show me the truth that sets me free.

August 16

WE LOOK AT YOUR HEART

I SEE YOUR HEART for Father, and that's what He's looking at. I see your heart for Jesus, and it moves Him. I see your heart for Me, and it delights Me. Man looks at the outward appearance, the flaws, the weaknesses—even the strengths—but We look at your heart. Your love may seem imperfect and weak toward Us in your own eyes, but it moves Our heart. It thrills Us.

We love you more than you know. As you grow in revelation of Our love for you, your love for Us will increase. We're looking at your heart. We're watching your heart grow in love. We're watching you grow in Christ. We love you.

PSALM 26:2; HEBREWS 10:22; 1 JOHN 4:16

→ PRAYER ←

I feel as if I fail You many times, but I do love You. Teach me how to love You more. Give me an anointing to love You more. Increase my capacity to love You more. You deserve all my love and even more than I have to give.

WALK IN PEACE AND POWER

WHEN YOU FIND yourself getting upset over any situation, check your thoughts. When you are upset by circumstances around you, you've stopped trusting Me. Where trust exists, peace flows. Where peace abides, power flows. Where power is present, change can occur.

Father wants to work all things together for your good because He loves you and You love Him. So cast your cares upon Him and pray. You will walk in peace and power in Christ—and you will see things change in time.

ROMANS 12:2; PHILIPPIANS 4:6–9;
NUMBERS 23:19

→ PRAYER ←

Your truth is powerful. Your Word is quick and alive, sharper than any two-edged sword. Let me be quick to discern the thoughts that don't line up with the truth that is in Your Word. Empower me to reject the lies of the enemy and the world.

August 18

A Revelation of My Love
Will Transform You

THE ENEMY WILL attack your identity—who you are in Christ—with suggestions that release shame against your soul. The enemy wants you to think there is something wrong with you, but I see you as complete in Christ. You are complete in Christ and accepted in the Beloved.

When people criticize, condemn, and judge you for areas of your character that are not yet perfected, refuse to receive the shame, guilt, and condemnation their words are intended to put on you. You are growing in grace, and I see you through the eyes of love. You will be transformed through a revelation of that love, not by man's criticism. Focus on My love.

COLOSSIANS 2:10; EPHESIANS 1:6; ROMANS 8:2

✦ PRAYER ✦

Thank You that I am free from the law of sin and death. I am a spiritual person and am judged by no one. Help me to reject the condemnation that comes from people and the enemy and to receive Your love, which helps me overcome every fault.

I Will Help You Forgive

*B*E QUICK TO forgive—quicker than quick. The longer you dwell on the sins committed against you, the longer you spend away from My heart, for My heart is a heart of forgiveness. I do not dwell on the wrongs done to Me. I do not dwell on the sins committed against Me. My heart seeks restoration. My heart seeks reconciliation. My heart seeks peace.

Dwelling on the sins committed against you won't yield restoration, reconciliation, *or* peace. Ask Me, and I will help you forgive both small offenses and great grievances. You just have to be willing.

EPHESIANS 4:31–32; COLOSSIANS 3:13;
MATTHEW 18:21–35

⊹ PRAYER ⊹

I am willing. I refuse to dwell on the sins committed against me. Empower me to be quick to forgive even those who hurt me the most—no matter how many times they hurt me. Give me a heart that seeks reconciliation and peace for Your glory.

August 20

I Am With You and for You

Tests and trials will come and go. But I will always be with you. Attacks and lies may come against you. But I am always for you. I am your secret place. I am your hideaway. No matter what comes your way, I am as close to you as you want Me to be. I can show you which way to turn and tell you what to say. I can direct your steps and put words in your mouth. I can give you wisdom and protection and deliverance. Everything you need I have, and I am willing to share it with you. Do not be afraid. I love you.

Romans 8:18; Psalm 34:7; Psalm 34:4

→ Prayer ←

No suffering I endure will compare to the glory that will be revealed in me at Christ's return. Thank You for standing with me through it all. Empower me to stand and withstand, and deliver me from evil, and I will glorify Your name on the earth.

TAKE THE LOW ROAD

You've heard it said, "Take the high road." In the kingdom of God it's not the *high* road but the *low* road you want to take—the path of humility. Taking this road means doing right by people who are not doing right by you. It means asking for grace and wisdom instead of moving in your own strength and intellect.

My thoughts are higher than your thoughts, and My ways are higher than your ways. Jesus is meek and lowly, a humble King who was exalted on high. I will help you walk in the grace of humility if you will let Me.

JAMES 4:6; 1 PETER 5:6; PHILIPPIANS 2:1–8

⇸ PRAYER ⇷

I choose humility. Will You pour out this grace in my heart? I choose to imitate my humble Lord. Will You give me the wisdom to walk in His ways? Help me to prefer others and honor others over myself.

August 22

FULLY SURRENDER TO ME

*I*F YOU WILL abandon yourself to Me, fully surrender to Me, and allow Me to completely have My way, I will so radically change your life for the glory of Jesus that everyone around you will bear witness to My transforming power and become hungry and thirsty for righteousness. If you will yield to Me at every turn, allow Me to renew your mind with the Word, and fellowship with Me day and night, I will give you in return more than you can imagine and will use you in ways you'd never think to ask. What do you say?

JOHN 15:14; ROMANS 12:2; 2 CORINTHIANS 3:18

→ PRAYER ←

I want to abandon myself, to fully surrender,
and to allow You to have Your way—but often
I miss the mark. Move my heart to meditate
on Your Word—and on You—day and night.
My spirit is willing, but my flesh is weak.

DRAW NEAR TO ME

*D*RAW NEAR TO Me as I am already near to you. I am always near to your heart. When you choose to draw near to Me and set your heart, mind, soul, and strength on loving Me, you will receive My presence, My love, My peace, My truth, My power, and everything else you need. My desire is for you to walk in close fellowship with My heart so I can truly direct you on the path to your destiny. Draw near to Me. I am already near to you. I am as near as you want Me to be. Come closer.

JAMES 4:8; PSALM 63:1–2; PSALM 42:1–2

✦ PRAYER ✦

I am hungry and thirsty for You, but the spirit of the world is always there to pull me in another direction. Strengthen my resolve to pursue intimacy with You above all things so that I can bask in Your glorious presence and lead others to Your heart.

August 24

I Am Always Faithful

I AM FAITHFUL. I am always faithful. I will not betray your confidence. I will not think differently of you no matter what you tell Me. I will not leave you without help. I will not hold back any good thing from a heart that seeks Mine. Whatever you need, I have it. When you need a friend, I am with you. When you need comfort, turn to Me. When you need understanding, I will provide it. I have so much to offer you, but many times you forget to draw from Me what you need. I'm reminding you—I am here for you.

1 Corinthians 1:9; Isaiah 41:13; John 15:15

✢ Prayer ✢

Holy Spirit, Your fruit is faithfulness. You are faithful, even when I am not faithful. Help me to draw from You everything I need to walk worthy of my calling in Christ and run my race in such a way that I will be counted faithful in the end.

Leave the Cares of the World Behind

*L*eave all the cares of this world behind. Don't take them on; reject them. This is our time of fellowship, and the cares and worries that enter your mind during our time together distract you from My heart. You cannot receive My peace, strength, joy, wisdom, and power when you are giving thought to the cares of this world. So once and for all, cast your cares on Me and look on Jesus. Keep your mind on Him. We'll take care of your cares—and take care of you.

Mark 4:19; Psalm 55:22; Matthew 6:34

→ Prayer ←

Sometimes the cares of this world do feel as if they are choking Your life out of me. Help me to resist the temptation to take on cares that You are willing and able to take care of for me. I trade my cares for Your peace, strength, joy, wisdom, and power.

Mercy and Goodness Follow You

*F*ATHER'S MERCY AND goodness follow you everywhere you go. Jesus's grace and love are chasing you. My part is to help you really understand that. Think about it: Mercy, goodness, grace, and love surround you. My power dwells in you. Christ in you is the hope of glory. When you truly receive the depths of these truths, when they become a reality in your everyday life, they will transform your vision, and you will see more clearly that mercy, goodness, grace, and love are enveloping you.

PSALM 23:6; COLOSSIANS 1:27; JOHN 16:13–15

→ PRAYER ←

*I declare that Your goodness and mercy
follow me wherever I go—and I rejoice in
this truth. Help me to recognize Your great
grace and mercy. Reveal to me the hope
of glory that dwells in my heart through
Christ, and I will praise Your name.*

We Have It All Covered

Sometimes you just think too much. Don't you know We already have everything figured out? Don't you realize We have a perfect plan that includes both the big picture and the small details? We have it all covered—every opportunity and every challenge. Instead of thinking so much about what could happen or how to do this or say that, try thinking about Father's love for you and Jesus's sacrifice at Calvary. Trust Me. I will reveal everything you need to know and do at the right time. We're on your side, and nothing surprises Us.

Proverbs 16:9; Ephesians 3:20; Psalm 32:8

⟿ Prayer ⟸

I'm so grateful that Your eyes are always on me and that You know the way forward. Help me to relax in that reality, to trust Your timing and leading. Order my steps along the perfect path that You have ordained for me to walk on.

I AM

*J*ESUS SENT ME to be your teacher, your helper, your Comforter, your companion, your friend. I am your Advocate. I fight for you. I am your counselor, and I offer wise counsel that will lead you into truth. I am your personal Intercessor, and I pray perfect prayers on your behalf. I am your standby, always ready to step in to help when you need Me. I am your strengthener. When you are weak, I am strong. I can strengthen you for anything that Jesus wants you to do. I am your healer. I am the revealer of truth. It delights Me to reveal truth to you and show you who Jesus really is.

JOHN 14:26; JOHN 16:7; 2 CORINTHIANS 12:10

✦ PRAYER ✦

*You are my everything. You help me in ways
I may never even know. I don't want to take
You for granted because You never take me for
granted. Teach me how to enter more deeply into
Your presence so that I receive all Your good gifts.*

RECEIVE OUR LOVE

I KNOW YOU ARE doing the best you can. Relax in Me. Your love may seem weak to you, but it delights Me. All I ever wanted from you was for you to love Me with all your heart, all your mind, all your soul, and all your strength. That is how We love you.

As you receive Our love for you, you will be able to love Us more and more and more. Your capacity to love people will also grow. And everyone will recognize you as one of Jesus's true disciples by the love you pour out. Let Us pour into you now. Are you ready to receive?

LUKE 10:27; 1 JOHN 4:9–12; JOHN 13:35

✦ PRAYER ✦

I am doing my best, but sometimes my best falls short—far short of the goal—and it's frustrating. Remind me to focus on You and Your love for me so that Your perfect love will overshadow the fears and frustrations that sometimes distract me from Your heart.

August 30

AGREE TO FOLLOW ME

*L*OOK AHEAD. WHAT do you see? Do you know that Father's plan for you is even greater than what you can see? Do you know that it was ordained long before you were even born? Do you know that no enemy is powerful enough to stop it? Although you cannot yet see the fullness of your destiny in Christ, you can move closer to it by agreeing in your heart and soul to follow where I lead you. It's My joy to take you there. Just agree.

PSALM 31:19; ISAIAH 64:4; ISAIAH 58:11

→ PRAYER ←

I know in part and I see in part—but I want to know more. Will You show me a glimpse of Father's plan? Will You lead me and guide me so that I will be certain to fulfill it? I will follow You.

YOU CAN FLOURISH IN THE FACE OF DIFFICULTIES

*I*F EVERYTHING IN life were easy, you would not grow into the character of Christ. Consider Jesus's time on Earth. Were the circumstances easy? Were the people around Him always supportive? Didn't the enemy come with temptations and stumbling blocks and persecution and betrayal? If the world hated Him, it will hate you. If people misunderstood Him, they will misunderstand you. No one ever promised it would be easy, but easy or not, you can walk in righteousness, peace, and joy in Me. You can flourish in the kingdom of God.

HEBREWS 5:8; JOHN 15:18; ROMANS 14:17

⟶ PRAYER ⟵

You never promised it would be easy. I know Jesus said there would be tribulation in the world. Will You strengthen me to stand in the midst of the world's hate? Will You help me move in Your joy despite the difficult circumstances?

September

For if you live according to the flesh, you will die, but if through the Spirit you put to death the deeds of the body, you will live. For as many as are led by the Spirit of God, these are the sons of God. For you have not received the spirit of slavery again to fear. But you have received the Spirit of adoption, by whom we cry, "Abba, Father." The Spirit Himself bears witness with our spirits that we are the children of God.

—ROMANS 8:13–16

Only Believe

Only believe. That's all that's required of you. Your deep belief, trust, and faith in Father will propel you into the good works Christ has prepared for you to walk in. By faith you will love. By faith you will fulfill the assignments We give you. By faith you will call those things that are not as though they already exist. By faith you will persevere when it looks as if all is lost. Only believe. That's all that's required of you. When you trust Me completely, everything else will fall into place.

Mark 5:36; Luke 1:37; Hebrews 11:1

→ Prayer ←

Increase my faith. Help my unbelief! Speak words of faith to my heart, and I will follow You. I will accomplish the good works Jesus has prepared for me as His co-laborer. I trust You; help me to trust You more and more.

September 2

HONOR ME WITH YOUR TIME

I APPRECIATE IT WHEN you adjust your schedule to spend extra time with Me. I see the demands on your time, the people pulling you in different directions, the pressures that try to crowd Me out of your day. When you honor Me with your time, I promise to help you meet the demands, the responsibilities, and the pressures the world brings your way. So come and take a few extra minutes with Me now. My grace awaits you.

JOHN 15:1–5; DEUTERONOMY 4:9; LUKE 12:34

❖ PRAYER ❖

*Spending time with You is a joy. I just wish
I had more time to give. Show me ways to
adjust my schedule so that I can spend more
time in Your presence, in prayer, in worship,
and in study. Give me the grace to do more in
less time so I can devote more time to You.*

DON'T LET THE ENEMY DISCOURAGE YOU

*D*ON'T ALLOW THE enemy to discourage you when things don't go the way you think they should—or work out the way you believe I want them to work out. He wouldn't bring discouragement to your heart if you weren't doing something he didn't like. He's trying to get you to quit doing what you are doing by making it look as if you're not making a difference.

You are making a difference to Me. You are making a difference to Father. You are making a difference to Jesus. You are making a difference to many people. Be faithful. Keep doing what you are doing. Your reward in heaven is great.

ROMANS 8:28; 1 CORINTHIANS 9:24;
GALATIANS 6:9

✦ PRAYER ✦

It does get discouraging to try my best and seem to fail. Thank You for encouraging my heart. Thank You for giving me the Word of God to encourage myself in You. Would You remind me that all things work together for good because I love You—no matter what the outcome is?

HOLD ON TO ME

*H*OLD ON TO ME because I am holding on to you. My hand of love has a tight grip on your soul. My grace can protect you from the enemies that seek to distract your heart from Mine. Your part is to receive My grace. Your part is to refuse anything that hinders love. Reject anything that causes you to stray from My heart or even look away from Jesus.

Hold on tight because there will be many distractions in the days ahead. My love is your safety net. I will never let go of you. Don't ever let go of Me.

JOHN 10:28–29; HEBREWS 13:5; JOHN 14:18

✦ PRAYER ✦

I will never let go of You. I am in You and You are in me. We are one. Show me if there is anything that is distracting me from Your heart, and strengthen me to hold on to Your Word when people and circumstances tempt me to let go.

STILL YOUR SOUL AND LISTEN TO MY VOICE

I HEAR YOU WHEN you cry out to Father. Do you hear Me when I cry out to you? Deep cries unto deep. The depth of who I am cries out to you with instruction, guidance, and wisdom. I am crying out to you with truth, revelation, and understanding. Sometimes you are so distracted by people that you do not hear My voice. But I am always standing by with what you need at any given moment. Still your soul. Listen to My voice. Heed My Word. I am speaking.

PSALM 18:6; 2 TIMOTHY 3:16; JOHN 10:27

→ PRAYER ←

Keep crying out to me, even when I am slow to hear. Keep speaking to my heart even when my soul is distracted. Give me ears to hear what Your Spirit is saying so that I will never miss Your instruction, Your revelation, and Your truth.

September 6

I Will Tell You What You Need to Know

You can ask Me anything. I may not always tell you what you want to know. I may not always tell you what you want to hear. But I will always tell you what you *need* to know and what you *need* to hear. I will never lie to you. I will never lead you astray. Though I do not reveal all I know at once, be assured that I will reveal truth to you little by little as you walk with Me toward your destiny. I will share with you what you can bear. So ask Me anything, and trust Me to tell you what you need to know. I am faithful.

Matthew 7:7; Numbers 23:19; John 16:12

→ PRAYER ←

I have many questions, but I know You have all the answers, so I am going to ask and keep on asking. Help me to be content with whatever You choose to share with me in Your wisdom and Your timing. I trust You to lead me into all truth.

MY LOVE FOR YOU NEVER CHANGES

I KNOW HOW MANY hairs are on your head. I know how many tears you've cried—and why you cried them. I know how many times you've stumbled. I know how many times you've wanted to give up. I know how many prayers you've prayed. I know how many praises you've sung. I've heard every word you've spoken, and I know everything you will say before you say it. Nothing you can do surprises Me—good or bad. And My love for you never changes. I see your end from the beginning, and it's just as beautiful as you are.

LUKE 12:7; PSALM 56:8; PSALM 139:4

✦ PRAYER ✦

You know me completely, and yet You still love me. This gives me great confidence in You. Thank You for comforting me when I mourn, picking me up when I fall down, helping me pray, and loving me through it all.

September 8

SEARCH MY HEART FOR SPIRITUAL TRUTHS

I KNOW ALL YOUR secrets. Would you like to know some of Mine? Would you like to know what is in the mind of Christ? Would you like to know what is on Father's heart? I will reveal the deep things to you if you seek Me. I know Father's deep secrets. Will you seek Me for His thoughts? Seek and you shall find. I want you to know the wonderful thoughts and plans Father has prepared for you. Search My heart for spiritual truths, and you will find what you seek.

DEUTERONOMY 29:29; PROVERBS 25:2;
1 CORINTHIANS 2:11

→ PRAYER ←

Yes, I want to know Your secrets. I want to know the mind of Christ and the heart of Father. Yet apart from You I can do nothing. Will You help me as I commit to seeking the secret things You want to reveal to my heart?

Look How Far You've Come

*L*ook back ten years. Did you ever think you would be where you are right now? Look how far you've come! Look how much you've changed! Look how your heart has grown! Look at the extent to which your mind has been renewed and how different your thoughts, words, and actions are. Look at what you've been delivered from and transformed into. Look at the victories you've seen in Christ. Look at where you've come from. Now, if you can, imagine where I can take you in ten more years. Take the limits off.

MATTHEW 19:26; LUKE 6:43–45; MARK 9:23

✢ Prayer ✢

I am amazed by how far You've brought me and how You've transformed my heart to be more Christlike. All things are possible to the one who believes. Nothing is too hard for You. Will You help me believe You for what looks impossible?

September 10

MAKE ROOM FOR MORE OF ME

*R*ECEIVE ME. RECEIVE more of Me. Make room in your heart for My truth. Make room in your heart for My wisdom, My gifts, My fruit, My power—make room for Me. Making room for more of Me means setting aside heavy weights. Set aside worry. Set aside the world's distractions. Set aside bad memories from the past that slow you down. When you let go of these things, you will be able to reach new depths in My love. I will shed My love abroad in your heart so that you can pour out that love to others for the glory of Jesus.

HEBREWS 12:1; PHILIPPIANS 3:13; ROMANS 5:5

→ PRAYER ←

I will decrease so You can increase. I will crucify my flesh so there is more room for You. I will die daily to the things of this world. I will deny myself and carry my cross. I ask only one thing as I set out to do this: give me grace.

KNOW THE SEASON YOU ARE IN

*I*T HELPS TO know what season you are in, for just as I told Solomon, there is a time to plant and a time to harvest, a time to tear down and a time to build up, a time to weep and a time to rejoice, a time to scatter and a time to gather, a time to speak and a time to remain quiet, a time for war and a time for peace. To everything there is a season and a time. I will reveal to you the times and seasons of your life if you ask Me. Your part is to stay close to My heart through them all.

ECCLESIASTES 3:1–8; 1 CHRONICLES 12:32;
PSALM 31:14–15

⟿ PRAYER ⟿

Your timing is perfect. Your seasons are purposeful. Please help me discern the seasons I am entering into and walking out of so that I can cooperate with Your Spirit. Please show me Your perfect timing in all things.

September 12

LET ME REVEAL CHRIST TO YOU

*J*ESUS SAID PLAINLY: "Come to Me, all who are laboring and heavy laden, and I will give you rest. Take My yoke upon you and learn from Me because I am meek and lowly of heart, and you will find rest for your weary souls. My yoke is easy and My burden is light." Well, how do you think you will learn from Him? He sent Me here to teach you. I am your teacher. I will reveal the depths of Christ's character—His love, joy, meekness, lowliness of heart, and more. Let Me teach you.

MATTHEW 11:28–30; 1 JOHN 2:27; JOHN 14:26

✦ PRAYER ✦

I want to learn of Christ from You. I want to learn how to rest in Him and how to walk in Him. Show me the depths of His character and transform me into His image, and I will never be the same. Teach me how to yield to You more.

Don't Let Emotions Lead You Astray

A soft answer turns away wrath. Peace begets peace. Wisdom holds its tongue when emotions are running high. We created you as an emotional being. We have emotions. We feel joy. We grieve. We get angry. But be ye angry and sin not. Be grieved and speak not rashly. There is a time to speak and a time to remain quiet and prayerful.

When I lead you to speak, I'll lead you with truth, grace, and love. That doesn't mean what you say will always be well received. But that's not up to you. As far as it depends on you, live in peace with all people.

Proverbs 15:1; Proverbs 29:11; Romans 12:18

✦ Prayer ✦

Emotions are fickle and unreliable. Help me exercise the fruit of self-control over my emotions—whether they're running high or low. Remind me of principles in Your Word so I can walk in truth, love, and peace no matter how I feel.

September 14

WE ARE LISTENING TO YOU

*Y*ES, WE ARE listening. Your heart's cries move Our heart. We have not only heard your prayers, petitions, supplications, and intercessions but also are actively working everything together for your good and the good of those you love. Our will is good, so trust Us without wavering. We hear your heart and it moves us. We are with you. Everything is going to be all right.

PSALM 34:17; 1 JOHN 5:14; PSALM 28:7

→ PRAYER ←

Thank You for listening to my heart's cries. Thank You for considering my petitions and acting on my intercession. I trust You. Help me to remain steadfast in trust even when I don't see the things I am praying about changing.

I Want to Bring You Into Deeper Intimacy With Christ

I WANT TO BRING you into deeper intimacy with Christ. I want you to grasp how wide and long and high and deep His love for you is. Nothing can separate you from it! He redeemed you with His blood, and you are His.

Meditate on the love of Christ. See Him as the Bridegroom king who burns with an undying love for you. Seek to understand His emotions toward you. Gaze on His beauty. Seek Him as Mary of Bethany and John the Apostle did, and you will hear His heartbeat. It beats for you.

PSALM 27:4; LUKE 10:38–42; JOHN 13:23–25

→ PRAYER ←

Holy Spirit, I want You to bring me into deeper intimacy. This is what I long for. Please give me wisdom, understanding, and revelation about the love of Christ. Please help me to keep my eyes fixed on Him and to lean into my Beloved's heart.

I Am Sharpening You for Battle

As iron sharpens iron, so one person sharpens another. Don't resist the iron. Don't run from the godly pressure. Don't try to escape the abrasion. It's all part of the process. Yes, Father has put people in your life as instruments to sharpen you. These people are not your enemies. So don't treat them like adversaries and opponents. Humble yourself and gain My perspective on the process. I am sharpening you for battle not against flesh and blood but against the real enemy: principalities and powers and demonic forces. I am sharpening you for spiritual war.

Proverbs 27:17; Psalm 144:1; Psalm 18:34

→ Prayer ←

I don't like the sharpening, but I know it's for my own good. You are training my hands for war and my fingers for battle. You are teaching me to walk in love and humility. I receive Your instruction. Please give me the grace to move through this season.

TREAT PEOPLE IN A GODLY WAY
EVEN WHEN THEY WRONG YOU

*D*O RIGHT BY people even when they are not doing right by you. Two wrongs never make a right, and you may be mistaken about the person you believe has wronged you. He may not have wronged you at all. The information you have gathered, the sense you have had, and the observations you have made may have led you to an incorrect assumption. And even if your discernment is accurate—even if someone is gossiping about you or maligning you or persecuting you—do right by him anyway. And pray for him. In other words, act like your Father in heaven.

GALATIANS 5:14; LEVITICUS 19:18;
MATTHEW 5:44

→ PRAYER ←

I don't want to assume the worst about people;
I want to believe the best. Help me. Strengthen
my heart to resist the temptation to trade evil
for evil. Give me the fortitude to return good for
evil and to pray for those who have wronged me.

September 18

Stand and Keep on Standing

I KNOW IT FEELS as if you've been waiting on the Lord for a long, long time. I know it seems as if you've been waiting for that change you are so desperate to see for ages. I know it looks as if your prayers will never be answered, but take heart. Be strong and of good courage. Know, trust, and believe. Stand and keep on standing in faith, nothing wavering. Do not grow weary in waiting. All of Father's promises are yes and amen. You will see the glory of the Lord in your situations. Keep standing. Don't give up now.

LAMENTATIONS 3:25; PSALM 27:14;
EPHESIANS 6:13

→ PRAYER ←

Thank You for encouraging my heart. I have done all I can do, so I will stand in faith, thanking You for Your good will. Help me not to grow weary in standing on Your Word and in believing for answers to prayer. I refuse to give up!

Give Your Ear to Me

*D*on't give your ear to the enemy, because if you allow him to whisper in your ear, before long you will be speaking his plans out of your mouth. You will give life to his deathly plans by coming into agreement with his lies. So don't give your ear to the enemy but instead give it to Me.

I desire to speak life to you, words of life that you can declare from your mouth in agreement with My will, words that will counter the enemy's lies and bring peace to you and grace to all who hear them. So give your ears to Me and your eyes to the Word, and your mind will be renewed.

John 8:44; John 10:10; John 6:63

→ Prayer ←

The devil is a liar, but he's so subtle that I sometimes entertain his voice when I should be casting it down. Help me to give my ear to Your words and Your words only. Help me to speak only those things that are in line with Your truth.

THANK GOD FOR WHAT HE HAS GIVEN YOU

*Y*OU DON'T NEED to pray for peace because Jesus already gave you His peace. You don't need to pray for grace because I, the Spirit of grace, dwell in you. You just need a deeper revelation of what belongs to you in Christ. He has given you all things pertaining to life and godliness. You need only to appropriate them. You need only to be mindful of what you have and thank Us for it. Thankfulness for His gifts of peace and grace unlocks the power to walk in them.

JOHN 14:27; JOHN 16:33; ROMANS 8:6

→ PRAYER ←

Thank You for Your peace! Teach me how to appropriate the peace You've given me. Teach me how to tap into that flow of peace that passes all understanding. Help me set my mind on You so that I can experience the peace that abides in me.

I Have Given You Gifts to Use for Christ's Glory

I'VE GIVEN YOU gifts, and I expect you to use them. I have given you natural talents that I want you to use for Christ's glory. I have also given you spiritual gifts with which to bless many. You have been called for such a time as this. You've been gifted for such a time as this.

Your gifts will make room for you. Look now for new ways to express your natural talent and your spiritual gifts, and I will show you where to go. You will find a warm welcome. But walk forward in humility and remember, We have given you everything you have in order to accomplish Our will.

1 Peter 4:10; Romans 12:6;
1 Corinthians 12:1, 4–11

→ Prayer ←

Thank You for the gifts and talents You have given me. I commit my heart to using them according to Your will and for Christ's glory. Will You show me ways to exercise these God-given gifts? Will You give me opportunities to glorify Jesus?

I Love You

THE TRUTH IS, I love you. I have always loved you. I will always love you. I love you with a sincerity of heart that drives Me to live with you, to counsel you, to comfort you, and even to convict your heart when you begin to stray from My love.

Father loves you absolutely. Jesus loves you with a passion. Our love is perfect. Our love will not fail you. Nothing will separate you from Our love. Receive Our love today.

ROMANS 8:31–39; 1 CORINTHIANS 13:8;
1 JOHN 4:19

→ PRAYER ←

Thank You for Your love. You loved me before I ever loved You—and You will never stop loving me. Give me an anointing to love You more— and to love the people around me more and more. I want my love to abound and increase.

I Will Tell You When to Respond

Sometimes it's not worth answering those who oppose you—and sometimes you must. Look at Jesus. Many times He set the Pharisees and Sadducees straight when they tried to trap Him with words. Can you imagine the pride that had to be in them for them to try to trap the Word of God with human words? Sometimes Jesus answered back. Other times Jesus said nothing in His own defense—even when His flesh and blood were on the line. So be slow to speak, and I will put words in your mouth and give you an unction when I want you to respond.

Mark 12:13–17; Mark 14:61; Luke 21:15

✦ Prayer ✦

*Give me the wisdom to know when to keep
my mouth shut and when to answer my
accusers. When You want me to speak,
please teach me what to say. Put the right
words in my mouth. I want every word
I speak to be according to Your will.*

September 24

I Love It When You Make Time for Me

So many people in the world—even those who call Jesus Lord—rush around tending to the cares of life and neglect the things of the Spirit. I am filled with joy because you make an effort to spend time with Me. It thrills My heart. I love it when you lay aside the things that try to pull your attention away from our time together—when you say "no" to those things and "yes" to My heart. I love it when you stop for even a few minutes in the middle of your busy day to say, "I love You."

Romans 8:5; Luke 21:34–35; Galatians 6:8

→ Prayer ←

I'll admit that the hustle and bustle of life—and the difficult circumstances that come my way—sometimes distract me from Your presence. Prick my heart when I am focusing on the wrong things so that I will turn my attention back to You.

September 25

PRAY FOR THOSE WHO
HAVE WRONGED YOU

I KNOW YOUR HEART is to be reconciled
with those who have wronged you. I know
you have forgiven fully and have no ill will toward
them. That's the heart of Father toward His creation. Your heart for reconciliation touches Us. But
those who have harmed you may still be in bondage
to their own bitterness and deceived by their own
hurts. So continue to pray for them. I love them
too. One day Jesus will reconcile everything.

MATTHEW 5:23–26; HEBREWS 12:14–15;
MATTHEW 5:44; COLOSSIANS 1:19–20

→ PRAYER ←

*I strive to maintain peace with everyone, but
not everyone wants to maintain peace with
me. I am concerned for their souls, and I lift
them up to You right now and ask You to pour
out the grace of forgiveness on their hearts.*

September 26

I AM AFTER YOUR HEART

I DON'T NEED ANYTHING from you, but I want something. I want one thing. Yes, there is one thing I am after. I am after your heart. And I will not be satisfied with a small portion. I will continue to woo you with My love until you have surrendered to My loving pursuit. I want your whole heart. I want it all. We want it all. We love you with all Our heart, beloved. Nothing can separate you from Our love.

PROVERBS 23:26; DEUTERONOMY 6:5;
ROMANS 8:38–39

→ PRAYER ←

I give You my whole heart. I will hold nothing back from You because You are worthy of more than I could ever give. Show me anything in my heart that is resisting Your love, and I will turn away from it and return to You.

PRACTICE MY PRESENCE

*P*RACTICE MY PRESENCE. Be mindful that I abide in you. Think of Me throughout the day because I am always thinking of you. When you consider My presence; when My being in your midst is foremost in your mind; when you meditate on Me, you will sense My life. You will flow in My grace, wisdom, mercy, love, kindness, patience, gentleness, and all that I am. Practice My presence. Be mindful that I abide in you.

PSALM 16:11; PSALM 27:8; JEREMIAH 29:13

✦ PRAYER ✦

I want to practice Your presence. Engage with my heart day and night and teach me how to be more sensitive to Your leading. I want it to be obvious to everyone around me that I have been in Your presence by the fruit that manifests in my life.

September 28

LET YOUR LOVE FOR ME OVERWHELM YOU

J AM NEVER CLOSER than when your worship moves you to tears. When your heart of love begins to overflow with tearful expressions, I know you have seen My glory; you have tasted My goodness; you have taken a drink from My fountain of grace. Your hunger and thirst are being satisfied, and you are being refilled, renewed, and recharged. Where the Spirit of the Lord is, there is liberty. I love it when your love for Me overwhelms you.

JOHN 4:24; PSALM 34:8; 2 CORINTHIANS 3:17

→ PRAYER ←

I long to encounter Your heart in a new way, to worship You in spirit and truth, to press deeper into Your love. Let this not be an occasional experience. Help me to press past my flesh and wandering mind to worship You completely.

FATHER WILL USE THE ENEMY'S ATTACKS FOR YOUR GOOD

I KNOW NOT EVERYTHING you've been through has been pleasant. But know this: Father has the wisdom to use even what the enemy has meant for your harm for His glory. He wills to use even the enemy's attacks to increase you, to strengthen you, to ultimately use you to help others. Father will repay you for every injustice you've faced if you will let Him. Put each one into His hands.

You will go through more times in the future that are not pleasant, but trust Father to turn them around. He will be glorified in your life. He will see to it. Trust Him. He is good.

EPHESIANS 1:11; GENESIS 50:20; ROMANS 12:19

✦ PRAYER ✦

It delights my heart that You can somehow turn tragedy into triumph—and use even bad days to build my character. Help me to embrace the trials and injustices, knowing that I will grow in patience and that You will work things out according to Your will.

I Want Your Whole Heart

Your worshipping Me does not change My heart for you. My heart always has been and always will be perfect toward you. I will never love you any more or any less than I do now. However, when you worship Me, it changes your heart toward Me. Every time you worship in spirit and in truth, it makes your heart a little more tender toward Me and brings you closer to My heart. It changes your soul and strengthens your body to chase after Me at each new level. I want your whole heart.

Ezekiel 36:26; Psalm 51:10; John 4:23–24;
Matthew 5:8

→ Prayer ←

Change my heart, Holy Spirit! Test my heart and my mind. Prove me and remove anything that hinders love. Purify my heart. Give me a believing heart that stands on Your Word. With my whole heart, I cry: answer me, and I will keep Your statutes.

October

Likewise, the Spirit helps us in our weaknesses, for
we do not know what to pray for as we ought, but
the Spirit Himself intercedes for us with groan-
ings too deep for words. He who searches the hearts
knows what the mind of the Spirit is, because He
intercedes for the saints according to the will of God.

—ROMANS 8:26–27

SPIRIT OR FLESH?

*B*EING ABLE TO discern spirits requires you to have a discerning spirit. Deducing, supposing, presuming, or otherwise guessing can be a dangerous exercise. Many times what you think is a spirit is merely the flesh.

Be cautious not to get out of balance in the spiritual realm. The flesh is at enmity with Me. I war against the flesh. Often what you are facing is not a spirit but someone's carnal nature rising up against you. The person's actions may or may not be motivated by a spirit. Always ask Me.

1 JOHN 4:1; 1 CORINTHIANS 12:7–11;
1 THESSALONIANS 5:21

✦ PRAYER ✦

I don't want to play guessing games in the spirit, so I need You to show me what You need me to see. Help me to stay in balance with the Word of God so that I don't open myself up to deception. Increase my ability to discern the spirits.

TRUST MEANS NOT HAVING
ALL THE ANSWERS

*T*RUSTING ME MEANS not having all the answers. I know you like to have everything figured out ahead of time, but it's not always necessary or even profitable for you to have all the answers up front. Having all the answers doesn't require trust.

Many things are going on behind the scenes that you don't see. Seeing those things would only distract your heart. I will lead you forth by peace. You will recognize My peace because it is spiritual, not soulish, and it is perfect.

PSALM 13:5; ISAIAH 26:3–4; PSALM 33:21

→ PRAYER ←

I like to have all the answers. I like to see the whole picture. But I choose to trust You, the One who has all the answers and sees the whole picture. Help me overcome my worries, my doubts, and my fears and trust You with all that I am.

THINK ABOUT WHAT JESUS HAS DONE FOR YOU

STOP AND THINK about what Jesus, your beautiful Savior, has done for you. He hung on a cross, naked, with nails in His hands and feet, bleeding, mocked, despised of men, to pay the price for your sins. He did it all for you because He loves you with a passion. He did it hoping to win your love.

When He won your heart, He gave you His name, His Word, His authority, His eternal life, His mind, and His Spirit. There's nothing Jesus would not do for you. He wanted Me to tell you that today, and He wants you to remember it every day.

HEBREWS 12:2–3; ROMANS 3:25;
EPHESIANS 1:3–12

→ PRAYER ←

Thank You for redeeming me, forgiving me, and making known to me the mystery of Your will according to Your good pleasure. Thank You for blessing me with every spiritual blessing. Help me to walk in the fullness of what Christ did for me.

October 4

LET YOUR SPIRIT MAN TAKE THE LEAD

WHAT YOU FOCUS on is up to you and you alone. And what you focus on sometimes seems bigger than it is. When you focus too much on a small problem, your mind begins to go down the "what if" path and determine possible outcomes. When you begin imagining how both sides of a difficult conversation will go, you are moving in the realm of the soul rather than the realm of the spirit. Father created you with a mind and an intellect, but He always intended for your spirit man to take the lead. A mind not at peace is a mind that is not submitted to Me.

PSALM 43:5; HEBREWS 4:12; ROMANS 8:6

→ PRAYER ←

I don't want to magnify problems. I want to magnify You. Help me not to engage in endless reasoning that leads me to worry and fretting. Help me to keep my mind off the things of this world and listen to what You are saying to me so I can have peace.

STAY HUNGRY FOR GOD

A HEART DESPERATE FOR Jesus is so beautiful. The sound of your worship draws Us closer to you. We are nearer to you than you think. You are Our tabernacle of praise. We've drawn near to you as you've drawn near to us. Precious moments of communion with you give Us an opportunity to share Our heart, fill your spirit, and bless your mind with a greater revelation of who you were created to be.

Stay hungry. Stay thirsty. Every encounter with Us will bring increase to your spirit. We are blessed when you receive Our blessing of intimacy.

PSALM 119:10; ISAIAH 26:9; PSALM 63:1

✦ PRAYER ✦

My soul longs for You as David's did, and I will not be satisfied with anything less than Your presence. Draw me into Your presence and show me Your glory. Give me a greater capacity to receive revelation about who You are, and I will seek You all the more.

October 6

WATCH OUT FOR THE LITTLE FOXES

JESUS, YOUR BELOVED, is watching over you with eyes of love. Here is His warning: It's the little foxes that spoil the vines blooming with His love. Watch out for those little foxes—the offenses and accusations the enemy brings against Him when you are experiencing trials, the wrong thoughts that distract your gaze from His heart, the idle words that lack faith. Watch out for the little foxes that eat away at your intimacy with Him.

SONG OF SONGS 2:4; SONG OF SONGS 2:15;
HEBREWS 11:6

✦ PRAYER ✦

Jesus is my bright morning star, the Alpha and the Omega, the Prince of Peace, my Beloved. Please help me rid the garden of my heart of the little foxes that choke out my ability to receive His love. Help me weed my garden.

GOD'S PLANS FOR YOU ARE GOOD

I WANT YOU TO receive this truth: Jesus has blessed you with every spiritual blessing. He handpicked you before the world was created to be holy and without blame before Him. He predestined you for adoption into Our family because He loves you. You are redeemed, reconciled, forgiven, and loved. Think about what each of those words means!

Jesus is preparing a place for you where you will come to know Him more fully. Even now, I am transforming you into His beautiful image, preparing you for that day. I want you to understand who Jesus is and who you are and to know all the kind intentions of His will. His plans for you are good. Rest in Him.

EPHESIANS 1:3–6; JOHN 14:2–3; PSALM 62:5

→ PRAYER ←

I receive this truth—help me to receive it more fully. I know who I am in Christ—help me to know more deeply. As I set my heart to meditate on Your words, renew my mind and show me the path to Your undisturbed rest.

WILL YOU LAY DOWN YOUR
LIFE TO BE CLOSE TO JESUS?

JESUS LAID DOWN His life to be by your side forever. Will you lay down your life to be closer to Him every hour? Jesus said that those who want to be His disciples must deny themselves, pick up their crosses, and follow Him. He said that anyone who loves his life will lose it and anyone who hates his life in this world will have eternal life.

Jesus declared that there is no greater love than to lay down your life for a friend. He calls you "friend." Will you lay down your life to be closer to Him now?

ROMANS 12:1; JOHN 12:25; LUKE 9:23;
JOHN 15:13–15

✦ PRAYER ✦

Yes, I will lay down my life. Like Paul, I consider myself crucified with Christ, and it is no longer I who live but Christ who lives in me. Help me to yield to Your perfect will in all things every day so that I will glorify the One who loves me.

Don't Dwell on Past Mistakes

*T*HERE'S NOTHING YOU can do about the past. There's not a person alive who has not made mistakes. Although it's good to learn from the poor decisions you've made, it does no good to dwell on them to the point of guilt, regret, and condemnation. You learn, in part, from your mistakes.

Pray for those you may have injured by your missteps, and release your concern about them. Repent for the trespasses that lie heavy on your heart. Then let them go. Commit to walking circumspectly before Me. Forgive yourself and move forward. You are not the only one who has made costly mistakes. But why keep paying the price forever? Repent and let them go.

1 John 1:9; Isaiah 43:25; Psalm 103:12

→ PRAYER ←

*I've let the devil beat me up about my short-
comings for too long—but no longer. I
choose to receive Your forgiveness and
walk in it. I choose to believe that You
have removed my transgressions from me
and that You remember them no more.*

CHANGE WHAT YOU DON'T LIKE IN YOUR LIFE

*I*F YOU ARE not happy with your life, change it. You have the authority to change what you don't like. You can change routines, schedules, habits, relationships, attitudes, activities, and anything else that doesn't fit in with your goals, dreams, and purpose.

The frustration you feel isn't going to go away unless you change something—either the source of the frustration, your perspective on it, or your attitude toward it. I am here, ready to help you realign things. But you have to make the decision.

PROVERBS 19:21; PROVERBS 16:9; PSALM 54:4;
HEBREWS 4:16

⤍ PRAYER ⤏

*I repent of complaining because Your Word
says to give thanks in all things and not
to grumble. Help me to prioritize my life
in a way that pleases You. Order my steps
on the path You have ordained for me. I
will not turn to the right or to the left.*

I AM ALWAYS FOR YOU

*I*F I AM for you, who can be against you? If I am for you, what difference does it make who's against you? I am always for you. Even when I convict you of sin, I am still for you. I still love you. That's why I bring conviction—to bring you back to My heart. And when flesh and blood or principalities and powers come against you with accusations, I will stand for you, by you, and with you. Trust Me. Don't defend yourself. I am your Advocate. I am always on the side of truth for I *am* the Spirit of truth. No one can stand against My truth.

ROMANS 8:31; HEBREWS 13:6; PSALM 27:1–3

→ PRAYER ←

*Thank You for always being on my side—
and at my side. Your truth is a shield,
and I will walk in it. Please help me to
remember that You are a very present help
in time of need so that I will turn to You
and not lean on my own understanding.*

Expect Good Things Every Day

START LOOKING FOR evidence of My love for you. Start looking for My blessings in your life. Start looking for the ways I am moving behind the scenes. I am always loving you. I want you to recognize and receive My love. I want you to be mindful and grateful so you can share My goodness with others who don't know Me the way you do. I want you to expect good things every day—and to declare My will over your life. Start looking, and you will see a new dimension of My presence in your life.

NUMBERS 6:24–26; JAMES 1:17; PHILIPPIANS 4:19

✦ PRAYER ✦

I know You are blessing me more than I realize. Help me not to overlook Your blessings, Your gifts, Your love, Your grace, Your anointing, and Your presence. Help me to catch You in the act of blessing me so that I will thank You joyfully.

You Know the Right Thing to Do

Sometimes the reason it's difficult to make a decision is not because the decision itself is difficult. It's because acting out the decision is difficult. Sometimes I see you hold back because you don't want to hurt anyone. That's the right heart, but follow Me and put the people involved in My hands. Obey Me.

Sometimes you hold back out of fear of the unknown. Follow Me. Obey Me. You are in My hands. You know the right thing to do. Discerning right from wrong is simple. Moving ahead seems difficult, but remember that I am with you. I will help you.

James 2:14–16; Isaiah 41:10; Hebrews 5:14

✦ Prayer ✦

Obeying You requires action because faith without works is dead. Give me the strength and courage to follow through on difficult decisions, especially when it comes to those closest to me. I want to please You more than I want to please people.

HUMILITY DOES NOT FIGHT
FOR ITS RIGHTS

Don't seek to protect yourself. Father is your protector. Love seeks not its own. I know it's difficult not to speak up or act out when people are trampling on your perceived rights. But a humble spirit gives up what it deserves. Humility does not fight for its rights.

Take your cue from Jesus, who laid down everything that belonged to Him for your sake. Father vindicated Him and blessed Him with more than He gave away. Father will vindicate you in the same way—but you have to get out of His way. Seek the path of humility and you will find what you really want.

Psalm 121:7; Philippians 2:8; Isaiah 54:17

→ PRAYER ←

Holy Spirit, give me the grace of humility. I choose to lay down my rights and humble myself as Christ did. I know that if I humble myself, You will exalt me over my enemies. Give me a patient spirit so that I will wait on Your vindication with peace.

Mornings With the Holy Spirit

WALK IN GOD'S TIMING

AITING ON THE Lord is almost a lost art in this generation of instant gratification. The culture has deceived many people into chasing the bright, shiny object that captures their attention—at any cost. But as for you, wait on Me. Wait until I show you how to move and whom to bring along. Set yourself apart as one who walks in Father's timing, not lagging behind but not rushing ahead. You'll find greater peace, greater anointing, and greater success if you wait on Us to show you the who, what, when, where, why, and how.

ROMANS 8:25; PSALM 37:7–9; ROMANS 5:1–4

→ PRAYER ←

I don't want to be impatient. Help me to manifest the fruit of patience in my life so that I will be an example to others who are watching as I wait for Father's promises and walk through fiery trials. I commit to waiting on You in every season.

October 16

YOU WERE MADE FOR LOVE

*Y*ou were made for love—so *love*! You were created to love Me—so love Me. Refuse anything that hinders love. Reject any voice that distracts your heart from love. Drink in My love, which is better than wine. Receive the love I am pouring out on you—and then pour it out on others.

There is more than enough love to go around. Be liberal with your love. Be lavish with your love. Be extravagant with your love. And remember it starts with Me. You love Us because We first loved you.

SONG OF SONGS 1:2; JOHN 13:34; 1 JOHN 4:19

→ PRAYER ←

Thank You for Your love. Teach me how to love better—how to love You better, how to love myself better, and how to love others better. I want to love the way You do. Help me to walk in love, speak the truth in love, and think loving thoughts.

ASK AND KEEP ON ASKING

WHEN YOU ASK Father for what He already wills to give you, He is delighted. There are some answers to prayer that He is holding back for just the right time. But there are other answers He desires to give now, in this moment: Ask Him for a greater revelation of His heart. Ask Him to show you His mercy. Ask Him to share His wisdom. These revelations belong to you, and they are yours for the asking. So ask and keep on asking because His well of revelation will never run dry.

MATTHEW 6:8; 1 JOHN 5:14; MATTHEW 7:7–8

⇒ PRAYER ⇐

Yes, I want greater revelations of Father's heart of love for me, and His mercy, and His wisdom, and His grace, and His strength, and His Son, and His glory. I commit to asking for these revelations and expecting You to answer.

Respond in the Right Spirit

*J*EALOUSY IS UGLY and causes people to behave bitterly toward you. Cain was jealous of Abel and murdered him. So don't be surprised when jealous people try to murder your reputation with the power of death in their tongues. Jealousy makes a man furious and vengeful. Envy makes the bones rot.

Who can stand before jealousy? Many times when people come against you, they have given themselves over to this work of the flesh. Respond with kindness and gentleness. Don't allow a wrong spirit to provoke a wrong reaction from you.

PSALM 6:4; GENESIS 4:8; PROVERBS 27:4;
GALATIANS 5:19–21

⇥ PRAYER ⇤

I agree with Your Word, and I commit to move in the opposite spirit when jealous and envious people come against me. All I ask is that You give me the grace to show compassion and mercy in the face of those who seek to do me harm.

COMBAT PRESSURE WITH GOD'S PEACE

*P*RESSURE WILL COME. The world brings demonic pressure that seeks to overwhelm your soul. I want to teach you how to recognize this strategy and resist moving in the negative emotions it produces.

Pressure may come from people. Pressure may come from circumstances. Pressure will come from spiritual forces. Don't receive it. Resist it. Rise above it. Walk instead in the grace and peace that reside in your spirit. Yes, combat pressure from the world and from the enemy with the peace of Christ that passes all understanding. It will guard your heart and soul.

PROVERBS 24:10; 2 CORINTHIANS 2:11; JAMES 4:7

✦ PRAYER ✦

Teach me, please. Teach me how to avoid the feeling of being overwhelmed and to embrace Your peace in the midst of the pressure. Help me not to cave in under the pressure of people, circumstances, or spiritual enemies and to choose the path of peace.

October 20

SEE JESUS AS HE REALLY IS

JUST LOOK AT Jesus. Meditate on Him and who He is. Don't look to the right or to the left. Keep your eyes squarely on Jesus, your Bridegroom, your King, your Savior, your bright morning star, your lily of the valley, your rose of Sharon, the lifter of your head and the lover of your soul, your healer, your deliverer, your vindicator, your everything. Jesus *is* everything you need and *has* everything you need. He defeated death for you. Meditate on His glory. It will renew your mind.

JOHN 3:29; PSALM 3:3; PSALM 18:2

→ PRAYER ←

Life comes with so many distractions and legitimate concerns that demand my attention. Yet You have the answers to every problem I will ever face. Will You help me to meditate on You and Your Word instead of on the distractions and concerns?

YOU ARE WHO JESUS SAYS YOU ARE

*Y*OU ARE NOT who your enemies say you are. You are not who the world says you are. You are not even who your friends and family say you are. You are who Jesus says you are. You are complete in Him. <u>You are holy and without blame before Him</u>.

You reign as a king in life. You can do all the things He's called you to do. You were created for good works. You are blessed, righteous, and alive in Him. You are an overcomer, more than a conqueror. You are His ambassador on Earth and a joint heir with Him. Believe it.

COLOSSIANS 2:10; EPHESIANS 1:2–4;
ROMANS 5:17

→ PRAYER ←

*I believe what the Word says about me,
but my actions don't always line up with
what I say I believe. I need You to help
me root out wrong ideas about myself no
matter where they come from. Please help
me to see myself the way You see me.*

October 22

THINK ABOUT THE THINGS
THAT CONCERN GOD

STOP THINKING ABOUT the things that concern you—the challenges, the problems, the mistakes—and start thinking instead about the things that concern Christ and His kingdom. I assure you that as you shift your focus off yourself and onto Him, He will turn His attention to those things that concern you. He has you covered. He has your challenges and problems figured out and is working all of them out for your betterment as you stay prayerful. So concern yourself with one thing—following Him completely—and trust that He cares about what you care about. He will not leave you helpless.

HEBREWS 13:6; ROMANS 8:28; PSALM 121:3

→ PRAYER ←

I don't want to be selfish. I want to be selfless. I am determined to get my mind off myself and keep my mind on You—and on helping people come to know the One who loves them. Will You help me stay focused on You instead of on myself?

DON'T TAKE OFFENSE WHEN
PEOPLE DON'T APPRECIATE YOU

*I*T'S WRONG WHEN people don't say "thank you" for the gifts you pour out and the time you spend praying for them. But don't let that offend you. Don't take offense. When you give, give as unto the Lord, expecting nothing in return—not even a "thank you." Father sees your heart and will repay you for the good He calls you to do.

Many people in these last days are ungrateful. But that's nothing new. Even in biblical times only one of the ten lepers Jesus cleansed returned to thank Him. If people didn't appreciate Him, don't be surprised when they don't appreciate you. But I appreciate you. Let that be enough for you.

PROVERBS 19:11; EPHESIANS 6:7; LUKE 17:11–19

✦ PRAYER ✦

Sometimes I feel as if I am being taken for granted, but I know You see and appreciate the things I do. Remind me that I am not doing things unto men to win their approval but unto God to please You. Let my heart be content with this goal.

I Want You to Experience a Deeper Level of My Love

*Y*OU REALLY HAVE no idea how much I love you. I want you to experience a deeper level of My love. I want you to taste and see Father's goodness and understand His heart of love for you. I want you to feel the weight of Christ's passion for you and receive a fresh wind of His love. I want you to be overwhelmed by Our love—lost deep in Our love—and to gain a new revelation of Our heart. Stay with Me a while longer this morning and meet Me again later tonight. We love you.

JOHN 3:16; ROMANS 5:8; GALATIANS 2:20

→ PRAYER ←

I haven't scratched the surface of Your love. Help me dig deeper. Help me to press into Your heart. Allow me to comprehend the breadth and length and depth and height of Your love for me.

October 25

Your Trials Are Only Temporary

I ASSURE YOU THAT the trials you face are only temporary. They will pass. Try to remember this: the trying of your faith produces patience and many other good fruit when you commit your heart to obey My Spirit and My Word. Gird up the loins of your mind and cast down those vain imaginations. Father is in control, and He will not allow more to come on you than you can bear. He has strengthened you for any and every trial you will ever face. He will never leave you or forsake you. Lean on Me. I'll bring you through to a better place. Only believe.

JAMES 1:2–3; HEBREWS 10:35–36;
2 CORINTHIANS 12:9

✦ PRAYER ✦

*Strengthen me in my inner man so that I
am able to endure the tests and trials that
come my way in this world—and to not
only endure but also rejoice in them. Change
my perspective on trials and tribulation so
that I respond according to Your Word.*

October 26

LET ME HAVE MY WAY

*J*F YOU LET Me have My way, you will ultimately get your way. It may not be what you are picturing in your own mind at this moment, but I assure you that if you yield to Me in all your decisions, you will receive what is in the mind of Christ and in the heart of Father. Father puts godly desires in your heart and then fulfills those desires. And I know the pathway to the manifestation of your desires! Let Me have My way, and you will ultimately get your way.

MATTHEW 6:9–13; EPHESIANS 5:17; 1 PETER 3:17

✦ PRAYER ✦

*Have Your way in my life! Have Your way
in my family! Have Your way in my city!
I subject my will to Your will in all things
and ask You to show me how to walk in
Your will at all times. I declare that You
are Lord over every area of my life.*

October 27

I LOVE TO PRAY WITH YOU

I LOVE TO PARTNER with you in prayer. I love to make intercession for you. I love to pray perfect prayers to Father on your behalf, knowing that you will rejoice when you see the answers rain down from heaven. It thrills Me. I love when your listening ear hears the will of My heart and prays it through in the natural realm. I love to see your Spirit-led prayers bring Father's will to earth as it is in heaven. Would you like to partner with Me in prayer right now? Together we can make history.

ROMANS 8:26–27; EPHESIANS 6:18; JUDE 20

→ PRAYER ←

You inspire me to pray. You help me pray. You teach me to pray. I'm so grateful that You pray perfect prayers on my behalf. Will You pour out a spirit of prayer on my heart so I will be compelled to pray with You more and more?

October 28

JESUS DIED SO YOU CAN LIVE

REMEMBER THIS TODAY: Jesus died so you can live. He was crucified so He can live in and through you to bring more lost souls into His kingdom. Remember what Paul said to the Galatian church. He had the revelation that he was crucified with Christ and that his life was no longer his own. He understood that Christ lived in him and that he lived his life by faith in the Son of God who loved him, died for him, and rose again for him. Have the same mind and walk in this truth.

GALATIANS 2:20; 1 CORINTHIANS 1:23;
1 CORINTHIANS 15:3–4

✦ PRAYER ✦

I want the revelation Paul had about the crucified Christ—and the risen Christ. I want to surrender myself fully to Him and live my life for His glory. Will You give me the grace to embrace the work of the Cross and bear my own cross as I choose to die to self daily?

LET'S WALK THROUGH THE DAY TOGETHER

HERE WILL BE many people and things competing for your attention today. Some of those people and things will try to pull you away from My heart—to distract you from My presence. Some of them will tempt you to respond in a way that does not glorify God. You don't have to give in.

As you move about your day, keep in mind how much I love you. Ask Me what I think about situations as they arise. Ask Me for help in overcoming challenges. Let's walk through this day together. It's going to be amazing!

MATTHEW 26:41; 2 TIMOTHY 2:22; 1 PETER 2:11

→ PRAYER ←

I know I'm not wrestling against flesh and blood, but the enemy will use people and circumstances to tempt me to walk in the flesh instead of following Your Spirit. Please help me not to fall for the enemy's tricks. Help me to follow Your lead.

October 30

CHOOSE THE RIGHT PERSPECTIVE

*Y*OU CAN CHOOSE your perspective. Your life experience has caused your natural mind to have one perspective. But you have the mind of Christ and the Word of God. They offer you Our perspective on the issues of life. The enemy will try to sell you his perspective on events that unfold in your life. Don't buy into his evil visions. Choose instead by your will to look at life through the lens of the Word and through the eyes of eternity. You'll be more joyful, wiser, stronger, and more powerful.

1 CORINTHIANS 2:16; GALATIANS 5:1;
ROMANS 8:7–9

✦ PRAYER ✦

Help me guard my heart diligently because what I allow into my heart shapes my life. I want my life to be shaped by Your Word and by Your Spirit. Please break in with Your perspective on things when I am not seeing clearly.

COME INTO ALIGNMENT WITH ME

Choosing to align your heart with My heart at the beginning of each day is one of the wisest decisions you can make when you awake. The enemy does not slumber, and he wastes no time in chattering to your soul about the cares of your life, often before you get out of bed in the morning.

Align your heart and mind with My heart and mind each morning. Cast your cares on Christ as they arise and know that your every need is covered. If I wouldn't think it, don't allow yourself to think it.

JOHN 8:32; 1 JOHN 5:4; PHILIPPIANS 4:8

✦ PRAYER ✦

The cares of this world come to my mind as soon as I wake up. Help me to refocus my heart on seeking the kingdom and moving in Christ's righteousness. Help me to reject the worrisome and overwhelming thoughts the enemy offers.

November

But as it is written, "Eye has not seen, nor ear heard,
nor has it entered into the heart of man the things
which God has prepared for those who love Him."
But God has revealed them to us by His Spirit. For
the Spirit searches all things, yes, the deep things
of God. For what man knows the things of a man,
except the spirit of man which is in him? Likewise, no
one knows the things of God, except the Spirit of God.

—1 CORINTHIANS 2:9–11

I AM YOUR HELPER

*W*HEN YOU GET busy or have a bad day and forget to visit with Me, I miss our time together. I look forward to our fellowship. Although I am always with you and always thinking about you and always interceding for you, I long to hear your voice telling Me what's on your heart and requesting My help. I am your helper, and it delights Me to help you. Remember, especially on the busy days and the bad days, that I'm here to help. I am always here for you, and I can turn your bad days into good days if you'll focus on My goodness instead of on the busyness and the badness.

JAMES 1:5–8; PSALM 27:13; PSALM 145:9

❖ PRAYER ❖

Your love touches my heart. It's difficult to imagine that You love me so much. Will You help me remember to ask You—the One who loves me, the One who delights in me, the One Jesus sent to help me—for Your all-sufficient grace?

I Love You in Your Weakness and in Your Strength

THE THINGS THAT bother you don't bother Me because I see the solution. I see the growth possibility for you. I see the opportunity for you to learn more about Christ. The things that bother you about yourself don't bother Me either. I see you through the blood of Jesus. I may convict your heart when you stray from love's principles, when you stumble into the works of the flesh, but I am not here to condemn you. I am here to point you back to Christ's grace and Father's forgiveness. I love you in your weakness and in your strength.

2 CORINTHIANS 5:17; EPHESIANS 4:24;
2 CORINTHIANS 12:8

⊹ PRAYER ⊹

Thank You for the gift of righteousness in Christ that allows You to see me blameless. Help me to see myself the way You see me so that I can rise up in my true identity instead of wallowing in self-criticism when I fail to walk in faith.

YIELD TO ME IN THE WILDERNESS

When you find yourself in a wilderness place, it's possible that I led you there to show you something about yourself. Or it's possible that you stumbled off My perfect path into a place of trial and temptation. You will discern the reason for the season when you stop fighting it and start yielding to Me. I will show you what you need to see and tell you why you are in the wilderness if you need to know. I assure you that I will lead you out at the right time. Yield to Me. Learn from Me.

HEBREWS 2:18; HEBREWS 12:11; PROVERBS 12:1

⇥ PRAYER ⇤

I don't like being in a wilderness place, but I understand that You have a purpose for every season. When I find myself in the desert, please help me to remember Your words. Help me to learn quickly what You are trying to teach me.

November 4

ASK ME TO SHOW YOU MY WAYS

WATCH ME MOVE in your life and in the lives of others, and you will begin to understand My ways. When you learn My ways, you will better understand My heart. When you better understand My heart, you will surrender more of your life to My will. My ways are higher than your ways. But you can learn how I move and discover more about Me by studying My ways. Ask Me to show you My ways. I will answer this desire of your heart with revelation.

ISAIAH 55:8; PSALM 18:30; PSALM 25:4

→ PRAYER ←

Holy Spirit, teach me Your ways. Show me Your ways. Help me to see how You move in my life and the lives of others around me. Pull back the curtain and let me see the way You move in wisdom, grace, kindness, patience, mercy, and truth.

Mornings With the Holy Spirit

DO NOT GROW WEARY IN WELL DOING

I SEE THE WEARINESS of your soul at times. The enemy comes to wear you out and wear you down. But do not grow weary in well doing because you will reap a great reward if you just hold on. All the trials, tribulations, and troubles are only temporary. Even if they lasted your entire life on this earth, they would be only temporary—and they won't last your entire life. Bear in mind that eternity awaits you, and heavenly rewards are yours. Keep pressing on in faith. Keep fighting to stay on course. I am here to help you, and I guarantee you it will be worth it.

GALATIANS 6:9; REVELATION 2:3; HEBREWS 12:3

→ PRAYER ←

Jesus endured and resisted the temptation to do His will even when it meant going to the cross. I'm so grateful He did not grow weary in well doing. Please give me an enduring heart and an anointing to keep pressing on despite any hardships I face.

GOD WANTS YOU TO ASK
FOR WHAT YOU NEED

FATHER KNOWS WHAT you need before you ask Him. But Jesus encourages you to ask because dependence on Father will bring you closer to His heart. He is your provider, and He will not hold back any good thing from you. No person or devil can keep you from receiving what Father wants you to have. Only you can stop the flow by not asking, by asking with wavering faith or wrong motives, or by giving up. Father's heart is open to you. Only believe and act on your faith every day.

MATTHEW 6:8; JOHN 14:14; JAMES 4:3

✦ PRAYER ✦

I don't always ask for what I need because I think I can make it happen on my own. Stir my heart to ask and keep on asking—and help me to ask for the right things with the right spirit. I want to ask and receive so my joy will be full.

PRESSURE MOLDS YOU INTO THE IMAGE OF CHRIST

AT TIMES AS I lead and guide you, you will feel constricted, pressed, squeezed, and stretched. That's because you've entered through the narrow gate. This gate puts you on the path to eternal life, but there is pressure along the way to remain obedient. Your flesh does not like it. The pressure helps conform you to the image of your beautiful Savior. Though it sometimes feels like more than you can bear, the pressure will not crush you or harm you in any way. It will mold you and shape you into the image of Christ. It will prepare you for the next level of glory I am bringing you into.

MATTHEW 7:13–14; ROMANS 8:29;
2 CORINTHIANS 3:18

✦ PRAYER ✦

Sometimes I feel pressure from the inside and pressure from the outside. Help me discern the difference between pressure from the enemy and pressure that will change me from glory to glory. Help me to cooperate with Your Spirit.

November 8

HOLD ON TO ME

When it feels as if everything around you is shaking, reach out to Me. Take hold of My hand. I will lead you back to the rock of salvation, to the hope that anchors your soul, to the peace that surpasses all understanding and guards your heart and mind in Christ Jesus. Hold on to Me because I am holding on to you. Everything around you may be shaking, but the righteous will never be shaken or put to shame. Those things that hold you back may shake loose, but you are standing on solid ground. Hold on to Me in the shaking.

PSALM 112:6; PSALM 62:2; PROVERBS 10:30

→ PRAYER ←

I'm so grateful that You are holding on to me and will not let go. Help me not to let go of You when the trials of life shake my world and try to steal my peace. Help me to hold on tightly.

I Enjoy Being With You

*D*o you know what I really, really enjoy? Just sitting with you. Just engulfing you with My love. Just watching the peace that comes over you when you feel My presence. It's those quiet moments when deep cries out to deep that I relish. During those times, the connection between us is strong. You know that I love you and I know that you love Me without either of us speaking a word. I enjoy you.

PSALM 42:7; LAMENTATIONS 3:26; PSALM 62:5

→ PRAYER ←

I enjoy Your presence more than words can express. You delight me. Will You help me reach that place of being still and knowing that You are God even when the hustle and bustle of the world around me is demanding my attention?

I Want to Give You More

I WATCH YOU AS you give, give, give. You give willingly to your workplace, to your family, and to the household of faith—and even to those who are not part of the household of faith. You give generously of your time, your money—and your heart. I love it. And I want to give you more to give. Receive from Me now the grace to keep on giving. As long as your giving is motivated by love, you will always have more to share with others.

2 Corinthians 9:7; Galatians 6:10; Luke 6:38

→ PRAYER ←

I know You love a cheerful giver—and I love to give cheerfully. Thank You for giving me seed to sow. Please give me more and more so that I can reach out to more people with Your love, Your grace, and Your provision.

FOCUS ON WHAT I'VE CALLED YOU TO DO

You ARE A vessel of honor. Father created you that way. Don't look at what others can or can't do. Don't be bothered by what they do or don't do. Don't be frustrated when those around you are not living up to their potential in Christ, even when it means you have to pick up the slack. I have given you gifts and abilities that are unique to your calling. So stay focused on what I've called you to do, and pray for those around you who are not grasping their roles as vessels of honor.

2 TIMOTHY 2:21; 2 PETER 1:10; EPHESIANS 4:1–3

→ PRAYER ←

*I want to walk in a manner worthy of my calling
in Christ, with humility and gentleness, bearing
with others in love and working for unity and
peace. Will You give me the grace to walk
as a vessel of honor and remain prayerful?*

November 12

I WILL NEVER LEAVE YOU

I AM ALWAYS WITH you. Even when you walk through dry seasons—even when you feel far away from Me—I am with you. You may not sense My presence. You may not hear My voice. But know this: I will never leave the one who loves Me. I will never forsake you. I will not leave you helpless and alone. I am ever praying for you. Yes, I am with you.

SONG OF SONGS 3:1; JOHN 11:6; PSALM 22:2

→ PRAYER ←

*Thank You for encouraging my heart
with the knowledge of Your presence
even when it seems Your silence is deaf-
ening. Please help me to examine my heart,
show me if there is any offensive way in
me, and lead me in the way everlasting.*

Don't Shrink Back From the War

*Y*ou are in a war. But the fight of faith is good. Don't shrink back from the war. Don't doubt the power that backs your faith. No matter how the principalities and powers and other wicked forces assault you, you remain more than a conqueror in Christ who loves you. And remember this: The Lord is a warrior. The Lord is His name. And you are His battle-ax. So stay ready for battle because you are in a spiritual war. You have the victory. All you have to do is enforce it.

1 Timothy 6:12; Romans 8:37; Exodus 15:3;
Jeremiah 51:20

✦ Prayer ✦

I will stand and fight the good fight of faith with the assurance that I win. Give me a greater revelation of the power I have in the name of Jesus. Open my eyes and show me the heavenly host that's fighting with me. Give me the strength to stand and withstand.

November 14

Your Love for Us Thrills Our Heart

I KNOW YOU LOVE Me. And it thrills My heart to watch your love for Me abound more and more. You love Me because I first loved you. Jesus shed His blood for you, and I shed My love abroad in your heart. Yet you have chosen to pour that love back upon Us with such sincerity of heart that it compels Us to enter a great exchange that allows you to receive more as you give more. We know you love Us. Your love thrills Our heart.

JOHN 14:21; 1 JOHN 5:3; JOHN 15:10

✦ PRAYER ✦

I do love You—I love You as best I know how. Would You help me love You more? I want to love You with a perfect love—the kind of love You have for me. I know my flesh and self-will get in the way, but I am committed to learning to love You more. Please help me.

DON'T WORRY ABOUT TOMORROW

*Y*OU ARE GOING to be OK. I know sometimes you get anxious about what the future
holds. But you don't have to worry because Father
holds your future in His hands, and His thoughts
toward you are good. Rest assured that He plans to
prosper you and not to harm you. He plans to give
you a hope and a future in His kingdom that is far
above anything you can even dream. So don't worry
about tomorrow. Our grace is sufficient.

JEREMIAH 29:11; PROVERBS 12:25;
JEREMIAH 17:7–8

→ PRAYER ←

*I believe You. You are good. I cast my burdens,
fears, worries, and anxieties about the future
on You. I commit to thinking hopeful thoughts
about the future You have in store for me. Please
give me Your grace to walk in confidence.*

LOVE BELIEVES THE BEST

ELIEVE THE BEST. Determine in your heart right now to think, believe, and speak the best about every situation and about every person—including yourself. I've noticed that you often think, believe, and speak the worst when you buy into the enemy's whispered lies. As a man thinks, so he becomes.

Life and death are in the power of the tongue. Love thinks, believes, and speaks the best at all times. Love bears up under everything and is always ready and willing to think, believe, and speak the best. I believe the best of you.

1 CORINTHIANS 13:7; PROVERBS 23:7;
PSALM 19:14

→ PRAYER ←

I am in agreement with Your counsel to think, believe, and speak the best. Your wisdom will help me shut down the enemy's schemes against my soul. Will You shed Your love abroad in my heart again so I can walk in this truth?

DETERMINE TO DO GOD'S WILL

Y OU CAN DO anything you set your mind to. But you will be better off if you do what I've set *My* mind for you to do. Don't follow your own wisdom. It will take you only so far. Man's wisdom apart from Me is often flawed. Depend on My wisdom, and you will walk in peaceful paths. Set your heart to follow My heart.

I know the mind of Father. He loves you and has a good plan for you. So be determined, but determine to do Father's will rather than your own, and you will always be pleased with the outcome.

1 CORINTHIANS 8:2; EPHESIANS 5:15–17; JAMES 4:15

→ PRAYER ←

I don't want to be wise in my own eyes, so I set my heart to follow You even when it looks as if I'm going the wrong way. Would You give me an ear to hear Your wisdom and know Your will so I can walk in them all my days?

November 18

FATHER IS YOUR PROVIDER

FATHER CAN SUPPLY all your needs according to His riches of glory in Christ Jesus. Your salvation provides for all your needs, including prosperity. Your part is to seek first the kingdom of God and His righteousness. Everything else you need will be provided for you as you put your hand to the plow—to the assignment—I have given you. Reject fear over financial provision. Reject a poverty mind-set, and receive words of life over your finances. Father is a God of more than enough, and He is well able to take care of you.

PHILIPPIANS 4:19; MATTHEW 6:33; PSALM 50:10

→ PRAYER ←

*Father knows how to give good gifts to me—
He owns the cattle on a thousand hills. I am
grateful that He is a good Father. Help me
to understand the financial principles of Your
kingdom—reaping and sowing—so that I can
walk in the prosperity Christ has offered me.*

MY LOVE IN YOU SHOWS YOU ARE CHRIST'S DISCIPLE

TREATING OTHERS THE way you want to be treated is not a difficult task—if you love yourself the way I love you. So take some time each morning to receive My love and allow Me to shed My love abroad in your heart again and again so that you can pour it out on others. People will know that you are Jesus's disciple by the love you have for people. So let Me love on you, love Me back, love yourself, and love others today. Father is rejoicing over you with singing.

LUKE 6:31; JOHN 13:34–35; ZEPHANIAH 3:17

✦ PRAYER ✦

I want people to recognize me as a disciple of Jesus, and that means walking in love even when people are not walking in love with me. Will You remind me to stop each morning to receive Your love before I enter into this unloving world?

November 20

YOU ARE OUR TREASURE

Do you not know that you are the apple of
Father's eye? Do you not understand that
you are Christ's beloved one? Do you not perceive
that I dwell with you all day, every day, always? You
are like a priceless jewel, a treasure I hold close to
My heart, a prized possession I do not want to do
without. Father gave Jesus as your ransom, Christ
bought you with His blood, and I have sealed you.
We will not let you go. Only do not turn away.
Keep your heart firmly fixed on Us. We love you.

ZECHARIAH 2:8; PSALM 17:8;
DEUTERONOMY 32:10

→ PRAYER ←

*Your words move my heart. I am overwhelmed
by Your love. Help me to keep my heart firmly
fixed on You. Remind me of Father's love for
me when I am feeling the stress of everyday life.
Reveal Christ's heart for me, and I will rejoice.*

Encourage Yourself in Me

$\mathcal{B}$e encouraged today. Let Me encourage your heart. What's difficult for you is not difficult for Me. Lean into My grace, and you will be empowered with everything you need. You are already equipped to meet every challenge that comes your way. You are an overcomer. I abide in your spirit, and I am greater than any enemy that comes against you. Know this and do as David did: encourage yourself in Me. I am with you.

1 Samuel 30:6; Psalm 23; Proverbs 30:5

✦ Prayer ✦

Nothing is too hard for You, and when I stay focused on Your Word and Your will and Your love, nothing is too hard for me. When the enemy comes against me like a flood, stir my heart to encourage myself in You and with Your Word.

November 22

PRESS IN TO PREPARE YOURSELF

*J*UST AS I gave the skill, ability, and knowledge to Bezalel to work on the ark of the covenant, I have given you the skills, ability, and knowledge to do everything I have called you to do. But you still need to hone your skills, exercise your abilities, and increase your knowledge if you want to continue making a difference in your sphere of influence. Don't be complacent in this hour. Press in because I have new assignments for you. Press in now to prepare yourself. I have need of you.

EXODUS 35:30–35; 2 TIMOTHY 2:15; 1 PETER 3:15

✦ PRAYER ✦

*I welcome any opportunity to serve You.
Please help me to rightly divide the Word
of truth and to be an effective minister of
Your gospel in my sphere of influence. Help
me to use the gifts and talents You've
given me to make an eternal difference.*

I Don't Hold Your Sins Against You

*D*ID I NOT give Samson the strength to defeat My enemies even after he turned away from My heart? When you sin, it grieves Me for a moment, but when you turn your heart back to Me in repentance, I rejoice. I don't hold your sins against you, and I won't withhold the power, gifts, or anything else you need to do what I've called you to do and defeat the enemies that set you up for a fall. I am on your side. I am always on your side. So do yourself a favor: stay on My side.

JUDGES 15; ROMANS 11:29; PSALM 118:6

→ PRAYER ←

You are so gracious and kind and powerful and forgiving! Please help me to remember that when I sin, You are ready to forgive—and lead me not into temptation but deliver me from evil. Strengthen my inner man to stand against the wiles of the wicked one so that I will please You.

November 24

I Will Give You Instructions

I HAVE THE BLUEPRINT. I have the plans. I have the keys. I have the pattern. Just as I gave David instructions on how to build the temple, and just as I gave Moses instructions on how to build the ark of the covenant, and just as I gave Noah instructions on how to build the ark that saved civilization, I will give you instructions on how to build all the things I've called you to build. I'll share the blueprint, the plans, the keys, and the pattern. Ask Me for instructions, and I will show you Father's plan in His timing.

PROVERBS 19:20; PROVERBS 4:13; PSALM 32:8

→ PRAYER ←

You are faithful to share Your plans with Your people, so I will wait on You to show me the plans for my future, to teach me the way I should go. Please help me to hold fast to Your instruction so that I will succeed in doing what You want me to do.

RETURN TO ME

I AM THE ONLY One who can truly satisfy your heart. So when you begin to feel discontent in spirit and soul, return to Me. Return to My heart. Come and fellowship with Me for a while. I am always willing and available to feed your hungry spirit with My truth. I am waiting and watching for you to turn your head in My direction so that I can refill you. I am ever waiting to hear you cry out to Me so that I can answer you. Don't wait until you feel dissatisfied and discontent before you visit Me. Come daily to My wells of encouragement and love.

MATTHEW 5:6; EPHESIANS 5:18; HEBREWS 13:5

✦ PRAYER ✦

I am crying out to You now. I hunger and thirst for more of You. Draw close to me and fill me again with Your Spirit. I am here with an open heart to receive Your encouragement and Your love. I need more of You.

November 26

I Give Grace to the Humble

I GIVE GRACE TO the humble. Who are the
humble? The humble are those who weep
and mourn over sin—and then ask for forgiveness.
The humble are the ones who ask Father for what
they need. The humble are the ones who answer
My call to fast and pray. The humble are the ones
who rend their hearts, weep and mourn over the
sin of a nation—and then stand in the gap for that
nation. My grace is sufficient for anything you need.
Pray for grace and then receive it with a humble
heart. I'm ready if you are.

JAMES 4:6; JAMES 4:8–10; 2 CORINTHIANS 12:9

✦ PRAYER ✦

*Thank You for Your grace. Thank You for the gift
of travail. Thank You for the privilege of standing
in the gap in intercession for people and places.
I trust You to pour out Your grace on my heart
now so that I will walk more humbly before You.*

RECEIVE MY GRACE TO COVER FLAWS AND FAILURES

*A*S YOU GET to know people better, you will begin to see their flaws and failures. They will disappoint you. Forgive them. It will become easier for you to forgive people as you get to know Me better. No matter how much time you spend with Me—no matter how well you come to know Me—you will not find flaws and failures in Me. I am holy. But you will find grace and love to cover your flaws and failures—and those of others in your midst—as you fellowship with Me.

MATTHEW 7:1–5; EPHESIANS 4:32;
COLOSSIANS 3:13

✦ PRAYER ✦

I know I am not perfect, and I don't want to judge anyone. Help me to avoid criticizing people who don't do things the way I think they should. Help me to be tenderhearted and kind to people, even when they treat me poorly.

November 28

ASK FOR THE DESIRES OF YOUR HEART

*W*HAT ARE YOU able to believe Father for? What do you have a difficult time believing Him for? I already know the answers, but I want you to consider the questions and confront the enemies of your faith. I want you to recognize the voices of doubt and fear that come to rob Father's promises from you. *All* of Father's promises are yes and amen—they belong to you in Christ. The Word is true, and He is able to do much more in your life than is recorded in the Bible. Jesus is Lord. Begin asking for the desires of your heart and refuse to bow to the enemy's faith-stealing tactics anymore.

MATTHEW 19:26; GENESIS 18:14;
EPHESIANS 3:20–21

→ PRAYER ←

*I can see some of the enemies of my faith.
Thank You for empowering me to over-
come them, little by little, as I meditate on
Your Word. I am asking You now for those
things I haven't dared to ask for in the past
I am asking for the desires of my heart.*

I Want a Deeper
Relationship with You

I want you to come closer. Closer! *Closer still.* I want you to be so near to My heart that you will hear not only My voice but also My heartbeat with unmistakable clarity; that you will feel My overwhelming love for you; that you will smell My fragrance. I want you to know Me the way I know you. I want a deeper, more intimate relationship with you. I want more heart-to-heart talks with you. I know you want the same things. I'll show you the way. Come closer.

Song of Songs 2:10; Jeremiah 31:3;
John 17:22–23

→ Prayer ←

I want to know Your heart. I want to smell Your sweet fragrance and experience Your love for me. Show me how to come closer to You, and I will press in. Show me what I need to set aside to experience Your presence at another level, and I will do it.

WILL YOU YIELD TO ME?

I CAN DO THE impossible through you if you yield to Me. What is impossible with man is possible with God. I am looking for someone through whom I can show Myself strong. I am looking for someone who will stand in the gap. I am looking for someone who will say, "Here am I! Send me." I am looking for someone who will be a faithful witness as Christ is. I am looking for someone like you. What do you say?

2 CHRONICLES 16:9; ISAIAH 6:8;
REVELATION 1:4–6

> ✦ PRAYER ✦

If You can use my life for Your glory, then use it. I don't feel worthy of the high calling You have for me, but I know You work through people. Will You equip me to do what You need me to do? Will You give me the resolve to yield to Your will?

December

For the one who sows to his own flesh will from the
flesh reap corruption, but the one who sows to the
Spirit will from the Spirit reap eternal life. And let
us not grow weary in doing good, for in due season
we shall reap, if we do not give up. Therefore, as we
have opportunity, let us do good to all people, especially to those who are of the household of faith.

—GALATIANS 6:8–10

CHOOSE YOUR COUNSELORS WISELY

*B*E CAUTIOUS IN choosing those from whom you seek counsel. Not everyone is a sound sounding board. Some saints' souls are marred by unhealed hurts and wounds, and they filter life's experiences through their painful pasts. The wisdom they have to offer, though well-intended, comes not from a river of healing, peace, and reconciliation but from a stream of resentment, bitterness, and unforgiveness. Remember that Our wisdom is first pure, then peaceable and reasonable. Learn to discern the difference between My wisdom and the words of wounded counselors.

1 KINGS 12:6–19; 2 TIMOTHY 3:16–17; JAMES 3:17

✦ PRAYER ✦

So many voices try to speak into my life! Help me to keep my lips sealed when I am around those who cannot offer pure counsel. Give me a wise and discerning heart, and help me to hear Your wisdom in the words of those who give me advice.

December 2

Lean Into My Heart

Lean into My heart. I want you to hear what I am thinking about you. I want you to feel what I am feeling about you. My heart is overwhelmed with love for you. Lean in and listen to My heart. My thoughts toward you are good, and My love for you is perfect. When you see yourself through My eyes—through the eyes of love and through the blood of Christ—you will more readily receive My love, love yourself, and love others. Lean into My heart.

Zephaniah 3:17; Isaiah 62:5; Psalm 147:11

✦ Prayer ✦

I want to hear what You are thinking about me and feel what You are feeling about me. Help me to perceive Your presence and sense Your heart of love toward me. Give me a revelation of this love as I lean into Your heart.

Perfect Love Casts Out All Fear

*D*ON'T ALLOW FEAR to be your first response to fearful news. When you see or hear things that trouble you, turn to Me. I will point you to the truth, and it will cause faith and love to rise up in your heart. When My truth, My faith, and My love rise up in your heart, they will protect your mind from the spirit of fear that is attacking your soul. When you are in Christ, there is no reason to fear—no reason at all. Ever. Perfect love casts out fear—all fear. Let Me give you a revelation of My overcoming love.

JOHN 14:1; JOHN 14:27; 1 JOHN 4:18

✦ PRAYER ✦

When I get bad news, when bad things happen
to me and the people I love, remind me that
You are with me. Remind me of scriptures
I can stand on to combat the fearful emo-
tions that begin to flood my soul. Remind
me that everything is going to be OK.

December 4

HOLD ON TO HOPE

*F*ATHER IS ABLE to use every bit of your bad day, every part of your past, every moment of pain and persecution you've endured for your benefit. Believe that with all your heart and soul.

Nothing you face is too much for you. You are an overcomer. Nothing you endure will shake you or break you when hope is the anchor of your soul. So hold on to hope through every bad day, through memories of the past, through painful experiences, and through persecution. Father is using everything in your life for your good.

GENESIS 50:20; ROMANS 15:13; ROMANS 12:12

→ PRAYER ←

I'm so grateful that Father can bring good out of bad. That's a miracle, and it is a truth that gives me hope. I will hope in Your love. I will hope in You. I will patiently hope. Surely there is a future and my hope will not be cut off. Will You stir hope in my heart?

Give Me Your Full Attention

I don't want to compete for your attention. So just for a few moments give it all to Me. Don't think about the errands you must run. Don't think about the phone calls you must return. Don't think about all you must do today. Just sit in My presence. The grace to handle your day is available as you need it. I am your grace. Fellowship with Me for a few minutes, and everything else will be much easier.

Matthew 6:33; Luke 10:38–42;
2 Corinthians 9:8

✦ Prayer ✦

I will sit in Your presence and rejoice in You.
Help me to put my mind on You during this
time and to lay aside the nagging cares of the
world so that I can seek Your heart and receive
Your grace. I am willing. Please help me.

December 6

SHAKE OFF THE DUST

*S*HAKE THE DUST off your feet. The enemy of your soul wants you to get stuck in the mud of rejection, fear, and unforgiveness. But that is not My plan for you. I am taking you to a broad place— your promised land. People and places along your journey will try to trip you and trap you in the enemy's quicksand. Don't look at the people and places. Don't look at the faces of those who stand between you and My will for your life. Just shake the dust off your feet and bless them as you live and move and have your being in Jesus.

MATTHEW 10:14; ISAIAH 54:2; JEREMIAH 1:8

✦ PRAYER ✦

Help me not to take the words of unkind people personally. Give me a heart to bless those who curse me and pray for those who try to hold me back. I want them to know You the way I know You.

December 7

Think About God

$\mathcal{W}$HAT WAS THE first thing you thought about when you woke up this morning? What was the last thought that crossed your mind before you fell asleep last night? Do you remember?

We want to occupy your thoughts. We want thoughts of Our love for you to flood your soul as you lie down and as you rise up. We want you to meditate on the Word day and night to ensure your success. We want you to talk about Us with others and share Our love with them. But you have to know Us first. Think about Us because We're thinking about you.

PSALM 63:1–8; PSALM 139:2; PSALM 1:2

✦ PRAYER ✦

I want what You want. Help me to consider what I am thinking about so that I can weed out thoughts that are not in line with Your Word. Remind me of scriptures that teach about Your love, Your mercy, and Your character. I choose to meditate on You.

December 8

EVERY DAY CAN BE AN ADVENTURE

I KNOW THE DAYS are mundane much of the time. It feels as if they are the same old, same old, same old, and you long for something new and different and exciting. But I tell you that every day can be an adventure if you will take the time to listen to My voice and follow Me. Praying and obeying lead to a life of holy excitement that fulfills holy desires. You have a part to play in turning the world upside down for Jesus. Pray and obey, and the mundane days will give way to thrilling days. Keep the big picture in mind.

MARK 4:26–29; MATTHEW 10:8; ACTS 17:6

→ PRAYER ←

I am ready to go on a holy adventure with You! I will pray and obey! Will You make it clear what You want me to do? Will You help me change my perspective so that I can see the way even mundane days fit into Your plan?

I Can Work Miracles Through You

*I*F I CAN work miracles for and through Moses and Joshua and Samson and John and Peter and Paul, I can work them for and through you. I desire to see My power manifest in your life to bring the "suddenlies" you've prayed for into reality. I desire to use you to help others receive the miracles they've cried out for. Study the accounts of miracles in the Bible, and I will begin to build your faith and help you appreciate the small miracles I perform from day to day that often go unnoticed. Embrace the realm of the miraculous.

1 CORINTHIANS 12:8–10; 1 CORINTHIANS 12:28;
MARK 16:20

✦ PRAYER ✦

*Although I seek first the kingdom of God
and His righteousness, I also desire to move
in the supernatural realm so that Your
name will be glorified on the earth. Stir my
heart and help me to develop faith for the
working of miracles according to Your will.*

December 10

All Things Are Possible

WHY NOT PRAY for what you think is impossible? Just change your thinking first. All things are possible for him who believes. All things are possible with Father. Nothing is too hard for Him. His arm is not too short to deliver. His ear is bowed down to you. He loves it when you approach His throne of grace boldly with prayers that ask for and expect what most people think is impossible—what most won't dare to ask. So see your impossibilities as possibilities in Christ and pray, ask, believe, and receive what Father has planned for you.

LUKE 1:37; HEBREWS 11:1–3; JEREMIAH 32:17

✦ PRAYER ✦

Your Word says that if I have faith as small as a mustard seed, I can command mountains to be cast into the sea, and they will obey me. Help me to line up my words with Your Word and to speak Your truth out of my mouth in faith. I believe Your Word.

ENTER INTO THE OCEAN OF MY PRESENCE

I WANT YOU TO enter into the ocean of My presence so deeply that you would drown if I were not there to meet you. You ventured out of the shallow water; you waded up to your knees and then your neck. But what I have for you is so deep, you will be fully immersed. No effort of your own will take you there or keep you there once you enter in. What I have for you demands letting go of all your life rafts and allowing yourself to fall deeply into My love with nothing but Me to catch you. I'm waiting.

1 CORINTHIANS 2:10; EPHESIANS 3:18; PSALM 5:7

❧ PRAYER ❧

My deep is crying out to Your deep. Take me deeper still. I will abandon myself in Your love and drink of Your grace. When I am troubled, reveal Your deep love and care for me. Show me the depth of Your loving heart.

December 12

I Will Help You Grow Stronger

I SEE YOUR WEAKNESSES. Do you think they bother Me? I am strengthening you little by little. As I watch you press in and press on every day, your perseverance blesses Me. Every right choice you make, every step you take in My will blesses Me. Even when all you can do is stand firm, your determination blesses Me. I am not focusing on where you are; I am focusing on how to get you to the next level. Where you are weak, I am strong. So lean on and depend on Me step by step and day by day, and you will grow stronger in Christ.

ISAIAH 41:10; EPHESIANS 6:13; EPHESIANS 3:16

✦ PRAYER ✦

You are my strength. In You I live and move and have my being. Please give me the strength to continue walking in Your Word. Please help me to make right choices in line with Your truth. I can't do it without You, but with You I can do all things.

Ask God for Whatever You Need

*J*esus made a path to the holy place for you by His shed blood. You were purchased with a price. And it's the Father's good pleasure to give you the kingdom. So approach Father's throne of grace boldly and ask for what you need. Father knows what you need before you ask for it, and He has good gifts for you. He wants you to ask because He wants relationship with you. So seek Father's heart. Seek His face. And don't be afraid to ask Him for anything. He loves you.

1 Corinthians 6:20; Luke 12:32; Matthew 7:11

✦ Prayer ✦

Father, I am coming to Your throne right now with boldness because I know You love me. You know what I need before I ask, yet I am asking You to help me. You see the problems, and You have the solutions. Please break in with power and help me.

December 14

EXPERIENCE THE POWER OF GRATITUDE

*T*HANKFULNESS IS A powerful spiritual principle. When you exercise thankfulness every day, you will begin to experience its power. So give thanks in circumstances good and bad. Thank Father after you pray. Thank Jesus for His sacrifice on the cross for you. Thankfulness lifts your soul, edifies your spirit, eases your worries, and builds your faith. So be thankful in all things and experience the power of gratitude.

1 THESSALONIANS 5:18; PSALM 107:1;
EPHESIANS 5:20

→ PRAYER ←

*Thank You. Thank You. Thank You. I will
thank You at all times, and Your praise
will continually be in my mouth. Help me
to maintain an attitude of gratitude despite
my outward circumstances because You
are worthy of all my praise all the time.*

PRAY LIKE A TRUE DISCIPLE

I ENJOY THE MINISTRY of intercession. I like listening to your prayers. I love watching you press in to see Father's will come to pass on Earth as it is in heaven.

Jesus taught His disciples to pray. His prayer is not a formula for answers to prayer, but it is a pattern for purposeful prayer that brings results. Open your Bible to the Lord's Prayer once again, and allow Me to show you how to pray like a true disciple of Jesus. You'll discover that the prayer enriches your personal petitions and intercession and unlocks Father's will in His timing—sometimes in ways you would never have imagined.

MATTHEW 6:9–13; MARK 11:24; LUKE 18:1

→ PRAYER ←

I want to be more effective in prayer. Will You teach me to pray? Give me revelation about the Lord's Prayer, and I will embrace it all my days. Show me what to pray for, and I will partner with You in prayer. Give me a spirit of prayer and an anointing to pray more.

December 16

KEEP A RECORD OF MY WORDS
AND YOUR PRAYERS

*M*Y CONVERSATIONS WITH you are holy even as I am holy. I never forget the truths I share with you. I always remember the prayers I've prayed for you. I record them all in My heart because I love you.

Do you remember our holy conversations? If you write down what I share with you and record your prayers to Me, you'll be inspired and encouraged when you see the things you've asked for come to pass. Write them down. Meditate on them. Reflect on past answers to prayer. Recording and reviewing our communication will fortify your faith and strengthen our relationship.

MALACHI 3:16; ISAIAH 49:15; HABAKKUK 2:2;
PSALM 17:6

⇥ PRAYER ⇤

Your counsel is always wise and Your motives
always holy. Help me to get in the habit of
writing down everything You say to me so
that when You answer my prayers, I will
have even more cause to praise You.

YOU WILL BENEFIT FROM THE SACRIFICE OF FELLOWSHIPPING WITH ME

THE TIME YOU invest in fellowshipping with Me may seem like a sacrifice on some days. And it may be difficult for you to transition from My presence into a world that is racing ahead with no regard for God or man. But know that during our times of fellowship I am gracing you to deal with that racing world. Because you have set your heart on Me, I am protecting you from the evil in the world's darkness. The time you invest in fellowshipping with Me may be a sacrifice on some days, but when you sow to the Spirit you reap many benefits, including everlasting life.

LUKE 18:1; PSALM 91:4; GALATIANS 6:8

→ PRAYER ←

Oh, how I love Your presence! I would sit in Your presence all day if I could. Will You help me to make the most of our time together? Will You help me to recognize the fruit of our fellowship and motivate my heart to put aside childish things?

I'M CALLING YOU TO A NEW LEVEL OF COMMITMENT

*Y*OU'VE BEEN CRUCIFIED with Christ. You were brought with a price. Your life is not your own. Lay it down and let Christ live through you—completely. You'll live a miraculous life if you choose this path. Pick up your cross, deny yourself, and follow Him. He's worth it.

I am calling you to a new level of commitment to Christ's cause. I am calling you to be a living sacrifice and a living epistle that speaks of Jesus. So choose the narrow path and reject the spirit of the world that tempts you to follow the lust of the eyes, the lust of the flesh, and the pride of life.

GALATIANS 2:20; 2 CORINTHIANS 3:2;
1 JOHN 2:16

→ PRAYER ←

*I choose right now to lay down my life and
let Christ live through me. But I know this
is a daily choice. My will alone is not enough
to walk this path. Will You strengthen
my spirit to rise up as a living sacrifice
to the One who sacrificed all for me?*

I Will Help You Abound in Hope

*F*AITH IS THE substance of things hoped for. I know sometimes situations look hopeless. It looks as if some of your family members and friends will never accept Christ. It looks as if the pressure will never let up. It looks as if your prayers will never be answered.

Be assured that Father is working to make all things beautiful in your life. He's always on time. Don't stop hoping. When you begin to lose your grip on hope in the face of circumstances, turn to Me because it is by My power that hope will abound in you.

ROMANS 15:13; ISAIAH 61:3; ECCLESIASTES 3:11

→ PRAYER ←

You've given me the gift of faith, and You've given me hope as an anchor for my soul. Therefore I have everything I need to believe even in the face of what looks impossible. Will You remind me of this truth when my soul struggles with hopelessness?

December 20

DON'T LET CONVICTION
STEAL YOUR JOY

I GIVE LIFE. I give liberty. And I am just in My convictions of sin, unrighteousness, and injustice. My convictions work to bring life, liberty, and justice to your soul. So when I convict you, don't let your conviction steal your joy. Don't let it press you down. Don't let it make you feel as if I am against you.

Realize that I have come to shine a light on those things that hinder our relationship because I love you. Get in agreement with Me. Turn away from the things I show you, and the blood of Jesus will cleanse you from all sin, unrighteousness, and injustice.

JOHN 16:7–15; ROMANS 8:1–2; 1 JOHN 1:9

✦ PRAYER ✦

Thank You for Your grace and mercy. There is no one like You. You are kind to me even when I am not kind to myself. Will You help me to be as quick to forgive myself as You are to forgive me when I fail to walk in Your Word?

SET YOUR WILL TO DO GOD'S WILL

*Y*our spirit is willing, but your flesh is weak. But where you are weak, I am strong. I can help you overcome your flesh. I can fortify your soul with My love.

Your will is powerful, but it is not as strong as I am. When you set your will in line with Me, you can overcome anything. It's not by might and not by power but by Me, the Spirit of God. So set your will to do My will, but depend on Me to help you walk it out.

Matthew 26:41; 2 Corinthians 12:9–10;
Zechariah 4:6

→ PRAYER ←

My flesh is weaker than I would like to admit, so I thank You for Your strength to overcome every weakness as I pursue Father's acceptable, good, and perfect will for my life. Help me to lean and depend on You and not on my own strength.

December 22

DO YOU WANT TO LIVE IN PEACE?

*I*F YOU WANT to live in peace, walk in peace, speak peaceful words, and think peaceful thoughts, then seek out what I desire. I am the Spirit of peace. If you set your mind on what I desire, then you will live in 'harmony with Me and put to death the sinful nature with its lustful desires. If you give Me the reins of your heart, you will live a life of abundant peace no matter what is going on around you.

ROMANS 8:2–6; PSALM 26:2;
2 THESSALONIANS 3:16

⇒ PRAYER ⇐

Yes, I want to live in peace. I crave Your peace. As I commit myself to set my mind on the things of the Spirit instead of on the things of the flesh, I expect to experience Your peace. I give You the reins of my heart and ask You to help me stay focused on You.

PURSUE LOVE ABOVE ALL

*L*OVE NEVER ENDS. It's all right to desire spiritual gifts, especially that you may prophesy Father's will to your generation. But pursue love. Spiritual gifts will one day cease, so if you spend your time focusing on spiritual gifts at the expense of pursuing love, you are losing out on eternal benefits. The faith to exercise My spiritual gifts according to My will works by love. So pursue love above all else, and trust Me to use you as I will.

1 CORINTHIANS 12:7–11; 1 CORINTHIANS 14:1;
1 CORINTHIANS 13:8

→ PRAYER ←

I want to walk in the supernatural but not at the expense of walking in love. Will You show me how to balance my pursuit of Your gifts—which prove Jesus is alive—with my pursuit of Your love? Will You let me manifest Your gifts for Christ's glory?

December 24

JESUS HAD YOU IN MIND

WHEN JESUS CAME to Earth to save the world, He had you in mind. When He walked the earth performing miracles of healing and deliverance, He had you in mind. When He was in the Garden of Gethsemane surrendering fully to Father's will, He had you in mind. When He hung on the cross to redeem you from the curse of the law—to become a curse for you—He had you in mind. And He has you in His mind and heart now. His love for you is perfect.

JOHN 3:16; LUKE 22:42; JOHN 19:30

→ PRAYER ←

I love You, Jesus. Thank You for paying the price for my sins. Thank You for delivering me from the power of darkness. Thank You for welcoming me into Your family. I honor Your sacrifice on Calvary and ask You to give me a deeper revelation of Your work on the cross.

RECEIVE CHRIST'S LOVE

*J*ESUS CAME TO seek and save those who are lost—and you are His favorite. When you received Christ into your heart, you received the hope of glory. Though He has ascended to Father's right hand, His work in your life is not done. He is ever making intercession for you, and He wants an intimate relationship with you.

One day you will see Him face-to-face and will become as He is. Until then receive His love for you—love that motivated Him to lay down His life for you. Honor Christ in your heart and with your lips. Be His witness in the earth.

MATTHEW 18:11; HEBREWS 7:25; 1 JOHN 3:2

⇢ PRAYER ⇠

Thank You, Jesus, for saving my life! Help me to glorify Your name on the earth. Empower me to reach others with the truth that sets them free. Give me the grace to be a living epistle. I commit to lifting up Your name in my generation so that all men will be drawn to You.

December 26

DON'T HOLD ON TO RELATIONSHIPS

Sometimes separations must come. A close friendship may last only a season, and though the connection in the spirit remains, the day-to-day connection ceases. Sometimes close friendships hold you back from where I am taking you—where I want to take you. Sometimes your friends aren't called to go where you are going. That doesn't mean you are leaving them behind; it just means you are obeying My leading. You will be reunited in the end. So don't try to hold on to relationships that I have ordained as seasonal. Hold on to Me.

ISAIAH 43:18; PSALM 32:8; PROVERBS 4:25

✣ PRAYER ✣

I want to have the friends in my life that You want me to have. Help me to let go of the people who are unknowingly holding me back from Your will or slowing my pace. Help me to release the people You are leading me away from.

YOUR PRAYERS MAKE A DIFFERENCE

*Y*OU DON'T ALWAYS see the impact of your intercessory prayers, but I do. I am telling you the truth: every prayer you release on behalf of your family, your friends, your nation, the lost, the church—every intercessory prayer you pray—is releasing Father's power on the earth. Your prayers release angels. Your prayers move My heart to move in people and situations. You may not be able to see a difference, but your prayers are making an eternal difference. Keep praying.

1 TIMOTHY 2:1–4; EPHESIANS 6:18;
EZEKIEL 22:30

✦ PRAYER ✦

I believe in the power of prayer. Lead me into deeper intercessory prayer for the things that matter most to Your heart. Give me prayer assignments that will bring Your kingdom and Your will to the earth. Give me persistence in prayer for Your will.

December 28

Be the Kind of Friend to Others That I Am to You

I am your friend. I am the friend who sticks closer than a brother. When your other friends and family don't understand you, I do. When your other friends are too busy for you, I am right here with you. If your other friends betray you, I will remain true.

Seek to be the kind of friend to others that I am to you. Be there for people. Walk with them through their storms. Edify them. Comfort them during their times of need. And always point them to Jesus. That's the best thing a friend could ever do.

Proverbs 17:17; Proverbs 18:24; Proverbs 27:9

✦ Prayer ✦

Thank You for being a friend to me—and for showing me what a true friend really is. Show me people who need a friend and help me to walk with them, edify them, and speak Your words of life to them. I want to be a true friend to many.

Embrace the Changes of
Pace I Bring Your Way

Don't hesitate to shake up your routine now and then when I send you new opportunities. A focused life is a powerful life, but be willing to make time for those special moments that come along now and again. Don't be afraid to step out of your schedule and step into something new. If I've brought it your way or if I am leading you into it, it's good. So much of life is made up of day-in and day-out routines. Embrace the now-and-then changes of pace I bring your way. They may be just what you need to get a fresh revelation.

Joshua 1:9; Ephesians 2:10; 2 Timothy 3:17

→ Prayer ←

Help me to be flexible enough to move when You are moving and to walk through the doors You are opening even when change seems inconvenient. I don't want to maintain the status quo for status quo's sake. I want to walk in the new things You have for me.

December 30

KEEP PRAYING FOR THOSE YOU LOVE

I LOVE THOSE YOU love even more than you do. I see how you hurt with them when they suffer. It pains My heart also. I see how you rejoice in their victories. I rejoice also. I see your concern for them and hear your prayers for them. Keep praying and keep loving, but know that We love them even more than you do. Through your prayers and acts of love, you are playing an important role in their lives. Even if they don't appreciate it, keep praying. We are working in their lives.

ROMANS 12:15; 1 TIMOTHY 2:1; GALATIANS 5:13

⤏ PRAYER ⤎

I know that You hear my heartfelt prayers for family and friends, and I thank You that You are working to make all things right in their lives. Thank You for listening to my cries of intercession, even for those who do not yet know You.

ARE YOU READY FOR THE NEW THING GOD HAS FOR YOU?

EHOLD, I DO a new thing. Are you ready to enter into the new thing Father has planned for you? Don't be afraid of the new things that come your way in the days, months, and years ahead. For no matter what happens—through the good times and challenging moments—I am always with you. I am your Counselor, your Advocate, and your intercessor. So go forth, My friend, because We are for you. You have the victory in Christ.

ISAIAH 43:19; ISAIAH 41:10; DEUTERONOMY 20:4

✦ PRAYER ✦

I can't wait to see the new thing You are doing in my life. Help me to remain patient and confident in You when things begin to change. Remind me not to fear when things seem to be shaking. I will set my mind on the prize in Christ.

EMPOWERED
TO RADICALLY CHANGE
YOUR WORLD

Charisma House brings you books, e-books, and
other media from dynamic Spirit-filled Christians
who are passionate about God.

Check out all of our releases from best-selling
authors such as **Jonathan Cahn, Jentezen Franklin**,
and **Kimberly Daniels** and experience God's
supernatural power at work.

CHARISMA
HOUSE

www.charismahouse.com
twitter.com/charismahouse • facebook.com/charismahouse

11843